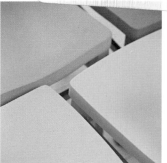

weekend furniture facelifts

Helen Carey

weekend
furniture facelifts

70 GREAT WAYS TO UPDATE YOUR FURNISHINGS

hamlyn

First published in Great Britain in 2005 by Hamlyn, a division of Octopus Publishing Group Ltd 2–4 Heron Quays London E14 4JP

Distributed in the United States and Canada by Sterling Publishing Co., Inc. 387 Park Avenue South, New York, NY 10016–8810

ISBN 0 600 61258 9
EAN 9780600612582

A CIP catalogue record for this book is available from the British Library

Printed and bound in China

10 9 8 7 6 5 4 3 2 1

In describing the projects in this book, every care has been taken to recommend the safest methods of working. Before starting any task, you should be confident that you know what you are doing, and that you know how to use all tools and equipment safely. Neither the author nor the publisher can accept any legal responsibility or liability for accidents or damage arising from the use of any items mentioned, or in the carrying out of any of the projects described.

contents

introduction

What kind of furniture needs a 'facelift'? Well, really anything that you have become fed up with or that is in need of some TLC, or any likely item you have spotted at a flea market or garage sale. These days, it's all too easy just to throw something away because you fancy a change, but look again – you may be about to lose that Moroccan-style dining table you have always fancied or a covetous set of dining chairs! Take a while to reconsider the piece, and browse through this book to see if there is anything similar: you will be thrilled if you can pull off a successful 'facelift'!

Don't think you can't do it – there is nothing simpler than painting a set of old chairs in candy pastels, and even creating a super-stylish mirror-topped dressing table is a breeze (see pages 24 and 84). All the projects in this book are skill rated: 'experienced' describes makeovers that are fairly tricky and best attempted after completing a few easier projects, 'confident' covers those that are not too difficult and just require you to go for it, and 'easy' means just that. I have also provided an estimate of the time each project will take, to help you plan your work.

finding furniture

So, what do you do if you don't have a house full of
tired old chairs or redundant tea trolleys? Hunting out
other people's 'junk' to make over is all part of the fun
and gives you an excellent excuse to spend many
happy hours browsing at flea markets, yard sales and
antiques fairs. Small ads in local papers can also be a
great source of material, as can the internet.

Don't go hunting with a specific item in mind, as
you will probably end up very frustrated. Perhaps
make a short list of projects you may like to do,
such as a chair, table or bookcase, or take with you
notes on areas of your home you would like to
improve – living room storage or bedroom lighting,
for instance. This way, you may see a piece that you
love and be able to rethink its purpose: a sewing box
to be transformed into a bathroom stool perhaps, or
a wardrobe into an armoire (see pages 130 and 20).
A little bit of planning should prevent you coming
home with 25 armchairs and a copper kettle (but I
can't promise it)! Searching out bargains can
become very addictive.

New furniture can also be transformed very
successfully. Simple wooden cupboards, glass-topped
dining tables and everyday utility furniture are just a
few of the items you can make your own. It
certainly doesn't all have to be junk, and sometimes
a new item has a better shape and feel. Preparation
time is usually shorter, too, although flatpack
assembly may be the exception that proves the rule!

choosing colours and materials

How should you go about choosing a colour palette, fabric and details for your facelifts? A good rule of thumb is to consider the eventual home of the piece and then choose a colour that will either blend with the existing décor (paler or darker in tone) or contrast with it successfully. A failsafe tool for deciding on a contrasting colour is the 'colour wheel' – any colours on opposite sides of the wheel will work well together as contrasts. So, sage green with terracotta, blue with yellow…

If you are undecided as to where the completed project will be placed, choose from a muted, neutral or natural palette. Creams, buffs and 'barely there' pale blues and aquas will work almost anywhere. There is always room for the odd wild card, though, so if you want a bright red painted chair with cut-out hearts stuck all over it, go right ahead! I did, and the finished item adds a real 'zing' to a pretty pale blue bedroom (see page 115). Even the most gorgeous neutral schemes will benefit from a little injection of personality, and there is no better way of bringing your own to a scheme than by adding one or two items you have made yourself.

Once you have decided on a colour scheme you can start adding other elements, such as fabric and decorative details – trimmings and hardware, for example. A plain piece of furniture can be brought to life by a beautifully patterned or textured fabric.

Think of the mood that you want to create and work from there. Do you crave country style? Florals and ginghams will suit. A neutral and natural scheme will work well with the addition of linens and suede-type fabrics.

More traditional patterns and fabrics include pretty Toile de Jouy and sumptuous velvet, which work well with classic interiors but also add a twist to a contemporary space. Search out interesting and beautiful handles, drawer pulls and trims. A crystal drawer pull adds a glamorous touch to a simple white-painted chest of drawers while decorative mouldings attached to a plain cupboard (see page 22) give a whole new look to a piece.

To make life even easier, there are an amazing number of new products to help you save both time and money. These include paints that cover almost any surface, safe and easy-to-use glues and paint-removal systems, and many new water-based products, paints and varnishes that are much more user-friendly. Take time out to browse the shelves of your local DIY stores – a new product may even provide the inspiration for a facelift you hadn't imagined before.

Magazines are a great source of new ideas, too, and if you can find any from another country these will provide you with a whole new approach. I keep a box file of cuttings, swatches and sketches so that I always have some inspiration to hand.

real recycling

I just love the idea of recycling a piece of familiar furniture into something you can fall in love with all over again. It's also hugely satisfying to be able to say 'I made that' — and at a fraction of the cost of buying new!

Quite often when stripping down an item to revamp I will be thrilled to find evidence of decades'-worth of makeovers — this is certainly not a trendy new pastime, and would have been a matter of necessity in days gone by. But before we get too serious, let's not forget that this book also includes an eyecatching coffee table made from delivery pallets and a bathroom chair clad in towelling (see pages 12 and 118)! Part of embarking on furniture facelifts is that there is lots of room for creating fun items, too.

As well as the step-by-step projects, at the end of each chapter you will find a gallery of ideas for that room, to provide you with extra inspiration for tackling lots more furniture facelifts. These include new storage solutions using anything from a wire rack in the bathroom to a letter rack for kitchen cutlery. You will see that with a touch of paint you can give anything a fresh lease of life. These galleries of ideas will help you really unleash the potential in everyday objects. So, invest in a bumper box of protective gloves, pick up that paintbrush (or needle, or glue gun...) and have fun!

livelier living

As the most heavily used spaces in our homes, living areas are also subject to the greatest wear and tear, especially in households with children. Replacing furnishings and accessories is expensive, and throwing out, say, a set of dining chairs just because they are looking a little tired simply feels wrong. In fact, they could look as good as ever with just a new set of covers and perhaps a little embellishment — and you can be proud of your recycling efforts. Plain wooden boxes could be made into more of a storage statement without losing any of their usefulness, while a battered old wardrobe can be born again to give you some extra shelving and storage space.

The current trend for perfect, neutral rooms looks beautiful but can lack personality. Pieces that you have worked on yourself will inject your own style, humour and taste back into a room. Why not start off with a lampshade or a mirror or two, and see where it leads?

pallet coffee table

Q **I would love to have a super-sized coffee table but don't have a super-sized wallet! Any suggestions?**

A This is a great solution. For the ultimate in utility chic, go no further than your local timber yard for two wooden pallets — the kind used for stacking goods for delivery. Teamed with nothing more than a large can of white sheen emulsion paint, they will give you a huge table that is bound to attract attention.

you will need
- Medium-grade sandpaper
- 1 litre (2 quarts) white sheen emulsion paint

tools
- Nail punch
- Hammer (if required)
- Pliers
- Power belt sander (or rough-grade sandpaper)
- Medium-sized old paintbrush

choosing materials

There are lots of other items that would also make an impressive oversized coffee table. An architect's plan chest works very well: these are often made in sections, from beautiful wood, and one section fitted with some large wheels to act as legs would be stunning. Alternatively, with the simple addition of four legs, a beautiful gilded picture frame can support a glass top that would look perfect in a classically themed space, as would an old tin trunk painted bright red in a modern environment. Making your own 'wow factor' coffee table like this will create a unique focal point for your room.

skill level
easy

colour palette
white/neutral/bright

time taken
2 hours

making the table

1 Check the pallets for protruding nails, loose staples or anything else that could cause injury. Use a punch (and hammer if necessary) to bang the nails below the surface of the wood, pliers to remove any staples or loose nails that you may find, and sandpaper to smooth any rough edges. The whole effect is fairly 'rustic', so you don't need to achieve a perfect surface. If you have one, a belt sander will give a great surface to the top pallet – as will rough-grade sandpaper and plenty of time and effort!

2 Hand sand any areas that you cannot reach with the power tool, using medium-grade sandpaper. This will ensure that you remove any sharp and dangerous splinters.

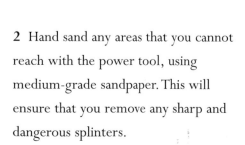

3 This is one time when you can dispense with primer. You are aiming for a beach-house, rustic look to this project, so just take your oldest paintbrush, put on a pair of rubber gloves and slap white sheen emulsion paint onto every surface. Simply stack one pallet on top of the other to create the finished table — there is no need to nail them together as this would make the table very heavy to move around. Add a selection of storage baskets and one or two brighter accessories to match the décor of the room.

etched-glass dining table

Q I have a new glass-topped dining table. I do like it, but it is a little dull. How can I make it more interesting while retaining the light and airy effect I love?

A A glass-topped dining table is a fantastic way to create a sense of lightness and space in a dining room. As an antidote to ultra-minimal living, using splashes of pattern and colour will create interest and prevent a room from looking bland.

you will need

- Dining table with removable glass top
- Wallpaper sample (one 'repeat' is enough)
- Masking tape
- Scrap paper or newspaper
- Glass spray paint

tools

- Scalpel blade or craft knife
- Cutting mat
- Tape measure

creating stencils

The vast range of wallpapers now available are a great source of inspiration for designing your stencil. Most stores will offer you a sample length for free, which should be enough to create your stencil. Larger patterns work best and are easier to cut out. Glass paint is available in smooth or frosted versions and even glitter effects. Practice is very important here to achieve a good finish – no matter how keen you are to complete your project, always try a few practice sprays on some bottles first. If you aren't confident making a stencil of your own design, and as a time saver, there is a wide selection of ready-made stencils available.

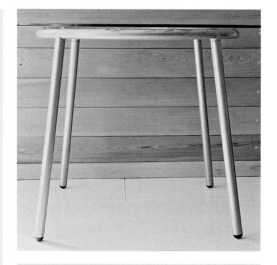

skill level
confident

colour palette
blue

time taken
4 hours

decorating the table

1 Using a scalpel blade or craft knife, carefully cut out your chosen wallpaper motif – remember that you are using what's left of the paper as the stencil, *not* what you are cutting out. A cutting mat is essential to protect your working surface, prevent slippage and avoid blunting your cutting blade.

2 Assess whether your table has a 'right' or 'wrong' side (see tip opposite). Clean the underside of the table really well to ensure that it is free from dirt and grease marks. Using a tape measure, find the centre of the table and mark with a tiny piece of masking tape. Position your first stencil to the edge of the table and in line with the centre mark. Mask off the surrounding area well, using scrap paper or newspaper secured with masking tape.

3

quick tip

A window or a decorative object (such as a vase) painted with glass paint, whether in spray or brush-on formula, is generally fairly hardwearing. Clean with regular glass cleaner and a soft cloth – just don't rub too hard. When a surface will receive a lot of wear, it is essential that the paint is applied to the underside of the glass. Most glass tabletops will be the same on both sides; however, you may find that yours has a bevelled edge and this will dictate a 'right' and a 'wrong' side. The bevelled edge will be the 'right' or top side.

3 Carefully spray on the glass paint. To ensure a good finish, start and finish each spray on the masking paper, *not* on the glass surface.

4 Peel off the stencil carefully to reveal the design. Continue building up your design, allowing each motif to dry before progressing to the next. How you position the motifs is up to you – it could be a random pattern or lined up in runs, as on a roll of wallpaper. When replacing the tabletop, it is essential to position it sprayed-side down – otherwise your design will wear off over time.

4

from wardrobe to display shelving

Q I am looking for some freestanding shelving for my living area. I don't want anything too modern as this wouldn't suit my home, but antique pieces are either too large or too expensive.

A A small wardrobe is ideal for transforming into a decorative 'armoire-style' shelving unit. Vintage versions are perfect, as they are smaller and have some decorative elements. However, a simple modern pine closet will work just as well.

alternative armoires

If you have a slim area to fill, you can decorate a simple bookcase in the same way. This would be ideal for displaying a collection of special china.

You may like the idea of an armoire but want to disguise the contents. Why not fit a pretty curtain inside the top of the front opening? Another good idea is to remove the wardrobe doors, cut out a centre panel on each one and sand the rough edges. Attach chicken wire to the inside of each door, covering the opening completely. You can leave this clear or add a fabric panel to the inside of each door. Then re-attach the doors to the armoire.

skill level
confident

colour palette
green

time taken
1 day

you will need

- Suitable wardrobe
- PVA adhesive
- Strong wood adhesive
- Decorative mouldings
- Panel pins
- Wood filler
- Medium-grade sandpaper
- Quadrant moulding, to make brackets for shelves – 1 for each side of each shelf, running front to back
- Small screws
- Paint or varnish stripper (if required, depending on the original finish – see step 6)
- 2–3 pieces of 1.25 cm (½ in) MDF (fibreboard), cut to size for shelves – measure accurately inside the wardrobe, then subtract 2 mm (⅛ in) all round
- 1 litre (2 quarts) primer (type depends on the original finish)
- 1 litre (2 quarts) green eggshell or satin finish paint
- 1 roll of wallpaper (for lining)
- Clear sticky-backed plastic (optional)

tools

- Hammer
- Filler knife or scraper
- Small screwdriver
- Mini spirit level
- Paint scraper (if required)

making the shelving

1 First remove the wardrobe doors and cover the whole of the inside with a thick layer of PVA adhesive – make a solution from 60 per cent PVA and 40 per cent water, as it is easier to apply. This acts as a sealant and a primer for the paint and paper finishes to follow.

2 Use strong wood adhesive to attach the mouldings to the outside of the wardrobe. They can be placed on the corners of the opening, towards the top of the opening on each side, and centrally at the top of the opening. Panel pins can be used on thicker mouldings such as shelf edging, but hammer them in carefully so as not to damage the delicate areas of moulding.

3 Using wood filler and a filler knife or scraper, fill in any holes left by removing hinges or others such as knots in the wood, and allow to dry.

4 When the wood filler has dried, sand it to a smooth finish. Check the rest of the surface and sand any other areas that may need attention.

5

6

quick tip

If you are confident with using a paintbrush, you could try hand-painting some swirls or flowers onto the armoire yourself instead of using a decorative moulding. Paper découpage, where a motif is cut from paper and pasted directly onto the surface (see page 68), would also be a pretty option. Wrapping paper is a good source of découpage motifs, although specialist designs are available from craft shops.

5 Cut the quadrant lengths to the depth of the shelves and screw the quadrants to the inside of the cupboard to act as shelf brackets. A mini spirit level and an extra pair of hands are essential here! Small screws are required, as you must avoid piercing through the wardrobe.

6 The wardrobe shown had already been painted, so I sanded it and then applied primer to unfinished areas such as the shelves and decorative mouldings. When the primer is dry, paint with one or two coats of eggshell or satin finish paint. It is easier to paint the shelves before fitting them inside the wardrobe.

7

7 Apply another generous coat of PVA solution (see step 1) to the inside back of the armoire. If you are using a heavy wallpaper, apply a coat to the back of the paper as well to ensure it sticks. Line the inside back of the armoire with pretty wallpaper, such as this silk-effect paper. Lining just the back adds decoration without being over-fussy. Line the base of the armoire with the same paper, folding each edge under to give a neater finish. Do not glue this down, as it may need to be replaced at regular intervals. If you want to avoid this, stick it down and cover with a clear sticky-backed plastic to make it easier to keep it clean.

prettier dining chairs

Q I have been given a set of dining chairs that I love, but they look a little 'heavy' in my home as I have an all-white colour scheme. It seems a shame to paint them, so how can I liven them up a little?

A Quite often something as simple as changing a fabric can work wonders on a piece. Here I've used Toile de Jouy fabric – a traditional French design that's back in style and can be found in pastel shades as well as striking monotones like this.

gold effects

The easy foil gilding system used here is a great introduction to the art of gilding. You can purchase all the materials for a foil gilding project in a handy kit from craft suppliers. If you enjoy this, you may want to progress to the more traditional gold leaf effect. To find out more, see page 88.

Other ways to pick out a detail in gold (or silver) include metal creams and waxes. These give a subtle effect that is actually the opposite to gilding: with a cream the gold effect will be in the recesses of the design, whereas with gilding the raised areas are coloured gold. You can also buy waxes in other metallic effects such as verdigris or copper.

skill level
confident

colour palette
monochrome/gold

time taken
1 day

you will need

- Dining chairs
- Sugar soap
- Very fine wire wool
- Restorative furniture wax
- Small can of rich red acrylic paint
- Pressure-sensitive adhesive
- 2 sheets of 'easy foil gilding' foil, each 12.5 x 22.5 cm (5 x 9 in)
- Foil sealant
- Approximately 0.5 m (¾ yd) pretty fabric, 145 cm (60 in) wide, to cover each seat
- Upholstery tacks
- Approximately 1 m (1¼ yd) braid, 1.25 cm (½ in) wide, to trim each seat (2 m/2¼ yd if you want a double row)

tools

- Medium-sized artist's paintbrush
- Scissors
- Fabric scissors
- Small hammer
- Glue gun

transforming the chairs

1 Scrub the chairs thoroughly with a weak solution of sugar soap. This old-fashioned cleanser is still used by decorators and is excellent for cleaning everything from walls and furniture to plastic storage boxes. It is suitable for all kinds of finishes.

2 Take a soft cloth and rub in a little restorative furniture wax to give the wood a lovely sheen.

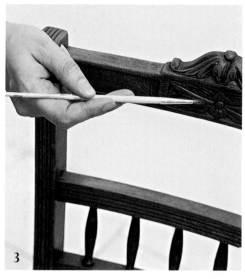

3 Pick out a small detail to gild. Don't be tempted to go wild here – this really is a case of 'less is more'. You can always add more gilding later if you want to. Using an artist's brush, carefully paint on a layer of base acrylic colour – usually a rich red, as here. Allow to dry.

4 Again using the artist's brush, apply a coat of pressure-sensitive adhesive. Once this coat turns clear, apply a second coat in the same way; when that coat has turned clear, proceed to the next step.

5 From a sheet of gold foil, cut a piece roughly the same size as the area to be gilded – this makes it easier to work with. Press on the gold foil, rubbing with your fingers and a soft cloth. Take care to apply the foil shiny side up: it's the dull side that is applied to the adhesive.

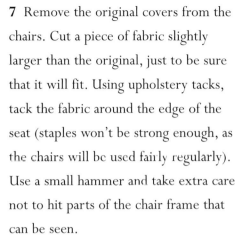

7 Remove the original covers from the chairs. Cut a piece of fabric slightly larger than the original, just to be sure that it will fit. Using upholstery tacks, tack the fabric around the edge of the seat (staples won't be strong enough, as the chairs will be used fairly regularly). Use a small hammer and take extra care not to hit parts of the chair frame that can be seen.

6 Gently peel away the backing to reveal the gilding beneath. Apply foil sealant over the foil to protect it and ensure that it stays on the chair.

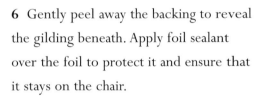

quick tip

Bear in mind the usage of chairs when choosing fabric. Should it be extra hardwearing or special-occasion luxurious?

8 To fit the fabric around the back of the seat, cut a diagonal line from the corner to the back strut of the seat back. Then firmly pull the fabric around it – the raw edges disappear down into the upholstery.

9 Using a glue gun, attach braid around the edges of the seat to cover the heads of the tacks. You can use one or two runs of braid to create the effect you want.

plain shade makeover

Q I adore decorative lampshades of all kinds – are they easy to make yourself?

A A plain lampshade can be customized very easily to match your scheme. This one has been dressed up simply and quickly with a smart combination of ribbon and lacing.

you will need

- Plain cylindrical stiffened-cotton lampshade
- Selection of ribbons, cords and/or leather thonging – approximately 1 m (1¼ yd) of each

tools

- Glue gun
- Eyelet punch and eyelets
- Fabric scissors
- Scalpel blade or craft knife

using found objects

Objects such as feathers and leaves can be glued onto a plain lampshade to great effect. Dried or skeleton leaves applied to a pale green shade or a duck-egg blue shade edged with a fluffy cream feather trim would both look fantastic.

skill level
easy

colour palette
neutral/coffee

time taken
2 hours

making the lampshade

1 Plan your design, then glue the first layer of ribbon trim to the shade using a glue gun. If you want to cover the seam on the shade, begin with that ribbon and then work on the more decorative elements, placing them where you like.

2 Measure a ribbon section to fit almost all the way around the shade, neatening the edges by gluing and folding over. Make a small incision near one corner of the ribbon using a scalpel blade or craft knife and push an eyelet through. Position the eyelet punch over the eyelet and squeeze firmly. Repeat near the opposite corner, and then at the other end of the ribbon. Then glue the ribbon to the shade.

3 Thread a piece of ribbon, cord or thonging through the eyelets and tie in a bow to create a corset effect.

quick tip

For a romantic feel, choose pastel ribbons and mother-of-pearl buttons; for a country room try gingham and ric-rac braid in cream and white. For a natural theme, look for wooden beads and feather tassels with which to trim your lacing.

Chinese print shade

Q I'm interested in making a shade from scratch, but can't source a frame locally and the postage costs for mail order are quite steep. What are my options?

A Battered old lampshades can be picked up for a fraction of the cost of a new frame. Just pull away the old cover and give the frame a good scrub – the bath is usually the best place for this.

safety first

It's better to choose a larger frame, so that you can use a low-wattage bulb and keep the fabric well away from it, avoiding any fire risk. If you are at all unsure, treat the fabric first with fire-retardant spray, available from shop-fitting or display retailers.

you will need

- Lampshade frame
- Approximately 0.5 m (¾ yd) Chinese print fabric, 80 cm (32 in) wide
- Matching sewing thread
- Approximately 1 m (1¼ yd) bias binding, 2 cm (¾ in) wide
- Masking tape
- Approximately 1 m (1¼ yd) bobble trim
- Decorative vintage or modern belt buckle

tools

- Fabric scissors
- Pins
- Medium-gauge sewing needle
- Sewing machine (not essential, but quicker)
- Tape measure (optional)
- Glue gun

skill level
confident

colour palette
multi-coloured

time taken
3 hours

making the shade

1 Cut the fabric length to run from top to bottom of the shade, adding a 4 cm (1½ in) hem allowance. Use the whole width of the fabric, as you will be gathering it up to fit the frame. Pin and machine or hand stitch the two side edges together to form a tube and press out the seam. Run two lines of loose running stitch around both ends of the tube to give a neat finish when you gather them in later. You can do this by hand, or on a sewing machine by choosing the largest stitches your machine will make.

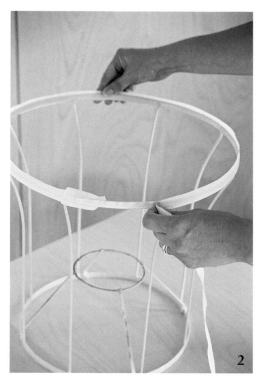

2 Carefully measure the top and bottom rings of the frame. You can do this with a tape measure or, even easier, using the bias binding itself. Use masking tape to hold the binding in place and help you to be precise, then cut it to length.

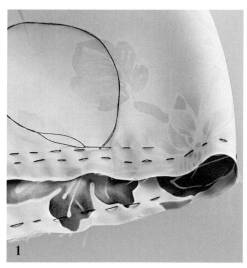

3 Pin one edge of the bias binding around the top of the fabric tube, adjusting the gathers as you go, then stitch in place. Do the same with the other length of binding at the opposite end of the tube.

4 Start at the top rim of the frame. Fold one bound edge of the fabric tube over the rim, pin and stitch securely using hemming stitch – make the stitches as small as you can. Then do the same at the bottom rim.

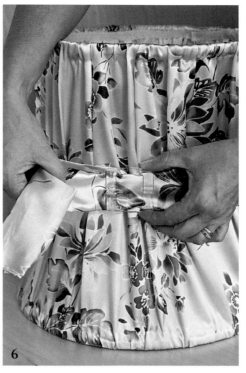

quick tip

A lampshade can be a useful tool for display. A collection of vintage brooches or a set of antique buttons will look lovely pinned or stitched to the shade. Use photo transfer paper to iron on old black-and-white family snaps or vintage postcards.

5 There's a wonderful selection of braids, bindings and trims available, and I couldn't resist these bobbles. Turn the shade upside down and glue the trim to the inside of the shade using a glue gun.

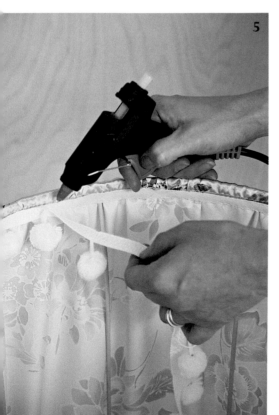

6 For a finishing flourish, make a simple 'belt' for the shade from a strip of the same fabric and a decorative belt buckle. This helps to give the shade shape and can be made into a feature, as here. Alternatively, you can treat it very simply with a band of fabric without a buckle, or even a piece of braid or cord.

tree branch chandelier

Q **I'm having people round for dinner next weekend and I only have bright overhead lighting. Any ideas for an instant, romantic light?**

A It's quick and easy to transform a tree branch and glass dessert or babyfood jars into a glittering country-style chandelier that will do the job beautifully.

ways with glass jars

Decorated glass jars make fabulous nightlights or votives. Punched paper or coloured tissue glued to the outside of jars will make lovely 'paper lanterns' – gorgeous hanging from trees in your garden. Tiny glass dessert pots painted with pastel-coloured glass paints and embellished with guests' names make sweet place settings for special occasions. Outsized jars half-filled with sand and a candle make great storm lanterns for outside entertaining or to place in a summer fireplace. Particularly pretty is to stand a line of jars along a table set for dinner. Half-fill each one with water gently coloured with food colouring, then float a candle or a flower in alternate jars for a simply stylish decoration.

skill level
easy

colour palette
white/pastel

time taken
2 hours

you will need

- Tree branch, approximately 60 cm (24 in) diameter from tip to tip, with lots of twigs strong enough to hang things from
- 1 litre (2 quarts) white emulsion paint
- Bunch of raffia or ball of white string
- Newspaper (optional)
- Plastic dust sheet
- Glass dessert or babyfood jars
- Glass frosting spray
- Cup hook
- Chandelier crystal drops, hearts and Christmas baubles
- Tealights – 1 for each glass jar

tools

- 5 cm (2 in) paintbrush

making the chandelier

1 Paint the whole branch with plenty of white emulsion. If you can suspend the whole branch from a length of raffia, you can do it all in one go; otherwise, lay the branch on some newspaper and do it in sections. Don't worry about being too precise with your painting technique as rustic is part of the charm.

2 Protect your working surface with a plastic dust sheet and then apply frosting to the jars, beginning and ending each sweep of spray away from the jar.

3 Make ties for the tealight lanterns from string or raffia. Wrap the raffia or string several times around the lip of the jar. Tie firmly and make a handle by running a loop of raffia or string up and over the top of the jar from the secured end, securing it again on the opposite side. Bind the top of the branch with raffia and create a loop from which to hang it, making sure this is secure.

4 Hang the branch in place from a cup hook and decorate with chandelier crystal drops, hearts and Christmas baubles. Place a tealight in each glass jar and add to the branch.

quick tip

Tealights are the only candles you can safely use for this project. Be sure to tie the jars securely and leave plenty of space above each one. Never, ever, leave a burning candle unattended. For a daytime special occasion, add a flower to each jar in place of the candle.

stylish toy storage

Q My children leave their toys all around the house. I don't want to keep them all in the children's rooms, but I do like clutter to be out of sight at the end of the day. Do you have any simple storage ideas?

A Most large DIY stores sell cheap kits for plain wooden boxes. These can be made over to suit any space, and with the addition of a padded seat will also provide some extra seating or a comfy footstool.

you will need

- DIY wooden storage box kit
- 1 litre (2 quarts) all-purpose primer
- 1 litre (2 quarts) terracotta eggshell finish paint
- Approximately 1 m (1¼ yd) thick wadding (batting), wide enough to cover the box lid
- Approximately 1 m (1¼ yd) hardwearing fabric, 145 cm (60 in) wide
- Approximately 1 m (1¼ yd) braid, 2 cm (¾ in) wide (optional)

all sorts of storage

These storage boxes are incredibly versatile and useful. To use in a hallway for storing shoes, cover the box with a heavyweight fabric to ensure it will wear well. A box can also be used in the bathroom for laundry – cover with a bright waterproof oilcloth. To tone with existing seating, you can easily cover the base of the box with fabric – PVA adhesive works well and prevents any snagging or scratching of flooring from staples.

Multi-tasking seating such as stools, benches and footrests create extra storage space and can be styled to complement your décor.

tools

- Paintbrush
- Fabric scissors
- Staple gun and staples
- Medium-gauge sewing needle
- Sewing machine (not essential, but quicker)
- Glue gun (optional)

skill level
easy

colour palette
terracotta/cream

time taken
1 day

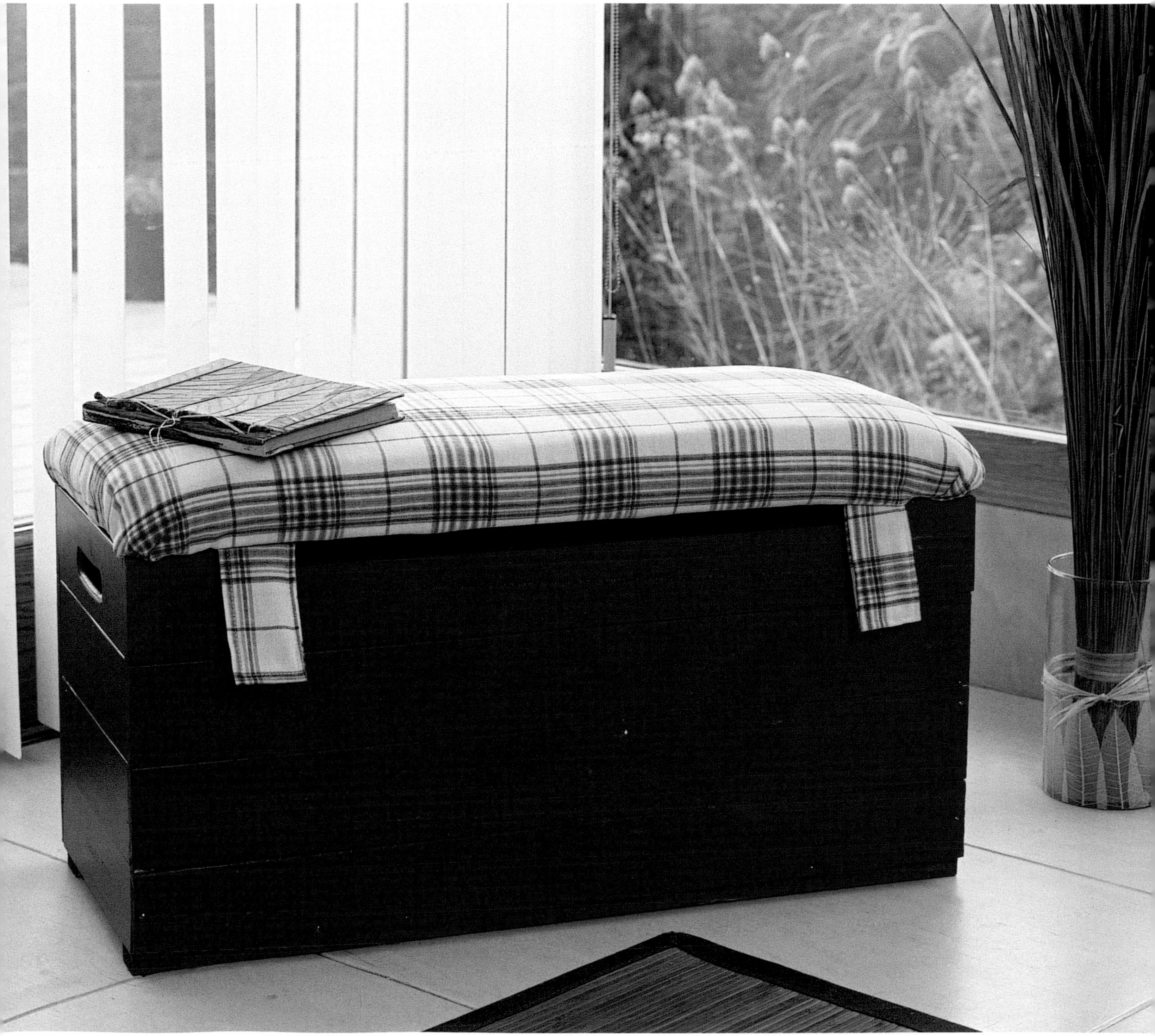

making the storage box

1 Make up the box according to the manufacturer's instructions. Treat the base with a coat of all-purpose primer, leaving the lid untreated.

2 Paint with a few coats of eggshell paint. It is preferable to use water-based paint here as it's so easy to clear up afterwards. A darker colour like this will need more coats than a paler colour – this piece took four coats to achieve the desired finish. When applying eggshell paint, it is best to work with a fairly well-loaded brush. Leave the lid unpainted.

3 Cut out three layers of wadding (batting), each slightly larger than the box lid to overlap and create a soft edge. Lay them on top of the box lid and staple through all the layers at each corner, right through to the wooden lid. This prevents the seat from moving around and also creates a softer, rounded edge to the finished seat.

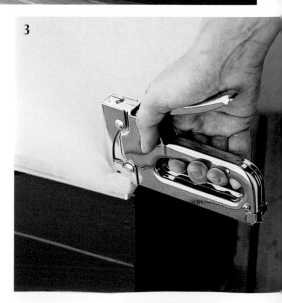

4 Cut out two rectangles of fabric, each approximately 35 x 15 cm (14 x 6 in). This will make a fairly chunky 'tab' — ideal for a toy box. Turn in both long edges so that they meet in the centre, fold the whole thing in two from top to bottom and then machine or hand stitch all around the edges to create the two 'tabs' to be attached to the lid later.

5 Cut a piece of hardwearing fabric to fit the lid, plus 10 cm (4 in) on each side just to make sure you have enough to work with. Place it over the wadding (batting) and fold under, then staple the fabric to the inside of the lid at regular intervals, keeping it as neat as possible. If you like, finish with a braid trim attached using a glue gun.

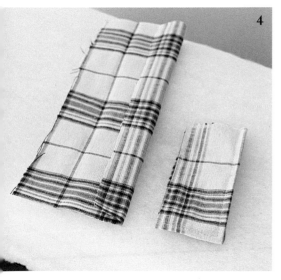

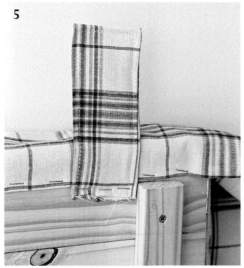

quick tip

Other ideas for pulls include loops fashioned from rope, plaited leather thonging or cotton tassels. If you don't want to paint your box, you will still need to protect the surface. A water-based matt varnish is one unobtrusive treatment; pale woodwash paints will subtly colour the wood, while keeping the grain visible.

6 Staple both pulls to the inside of the lid, giving you a neat and easy way to open the box.

skeleton leaves mirror

Q I've got a very plain circular mirror that I found at a flea market. How can I make it more interesting?

A This easy technique adds a delicate edging to a circular mirror. Skeleton leaves in subtle shades are very pretty and have an almost ethereal quality.

you will need

- Circular mirror, with pre-drilled screw holes for attaching to the wall
- Selection of skeletonized leaves

tools

- Glue gun (hot- or cold-melt works for this project)

alternative materials

There are many other items you could use to decorate a mirror in a similar way to the leaves used here. Alternative finishes might include silk rose petals or dried rose buds for a soft, pretty effect. Fresh ivy would be fun for a seasonal Christmas display.

skill level
easy

colour palette
neutral/mauve

time taken
1 hour

decorating the mirror

1 Decide where the leaves will sit on the frame of the mirror. I chose a layered effect for these leaves, but smaller leaves arranged in a sunburst effect would also work well.

2 Begin gluing the leaves onto the mirror using a glue gun. Place a dab of glue on the mirror surface and press the leaf onto the glue – trying to put the glue on the leaf is far too tricky.

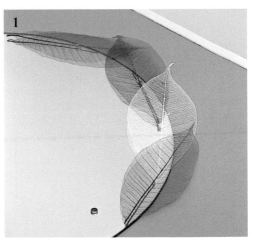

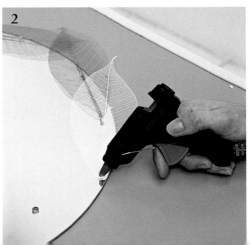

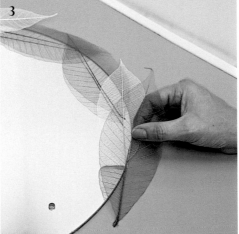

3 Build up the design on each side of the mirror at the same time, placing one leaf on the left and then one on the right, and so on, rather than working all the way around in one go, as this will create a more harmonious finished effect.

livelier living gallery

1 Mosaic side table

Mosaic tiles are available in all manner of wonderful effects. I bought this pebble-effect mosaic from a large DIY store, supplied in easy-to-use 30-cm (12-in) square web-backed pieces. Sand the table and paint with a soft seaside shade. Apply the mosaic tiles in the usual way, using a dual-purpose tile adhesive/grout. I like to leave a softer, more organic-shaped edge, but if you prefer a neater effect tack some beading around the edge of the tabletop before you tile.

2 Button mosaic photo frame

Use mother-of-pearl and vintage buttons to create a unique frame. This is a lovely way to use up all the odd buttons you have collected over the years. To attach the buttons, use a dual-purpose tile adhesive/grout applied with a medium-sized artist's brush. Wipe off the excess just before it sets – too soon and you will loosen the buttons; too late and it is difficult to clean away the excess from any detailing.

3 Wallpaper in a cupboard

Don't live with dull closets! If you are lucky enough to find a roll of vintage wallpaper that you love but wouldn't really consider for a wall, a hallway cupboard or cloakroom is a great place to use it.

4 Wallpaper storage boxes

If you have lots of clutter and paperwork on the go, cover a couple of shoeboxes with the same paper you have used on your walls. This is a simple way to streamline storage so that it blends with your décor.

5 Wallpaper in a frame

Another idea for using vintage or expensive papers is to frame a length like this. Many stores will offer you a sample length for free – you may even love it enough to go back for enough to paper the whole room.

6 Wallpaper under a glass tabletop

Wallpaper is a fun way of ringing the changes with a glass-topped dining table for a special occasion. Simply attach the paper with double-sided adhesive tape that can be removed easily with white spirit or lighter fuel.

7 Tapestry-style chair

This folding chair would originally have been slung with carpet. Here, this has been replaced with a modern tapestry-style fabric, making it pretty and strong at the same time.

8 Satin-and-pompom cushion

A design classic, invented by Gebruder Thonet in 1859, bentwood chairs can often be found at flea markets as well as modern furniture stores. This old one was given a coat of furniture paint and teamed with a jaunty cushion, made from a patterned curtain fabric finished with some fun pompoms for an 'Aladdin' touch! A group of these in different colours would make a wonderfully eclectic dining set.

9 Chair with crochet cushion

This version is teamed with a jaunty cushion made from an old crocheted blanket. You could also use knitted blankets or even old sweaters – Aran styles work particularly well when converted to cushions.

10 Sideboard with baskets

Sideboards are making a comeback as many people realize that they simply don't have enough storage. You may not want the traditional china and cutlery storage, though, so here an old sideboard has been revamped with a few coats of cream paint while large baskets fit perfectly where the doors once were.

11 Moroccan-style dining table

This shabby old dining table was cut down and given a distressed paint finish. Teamed with lots of cushions, it becomes a great low dining or coffee table.

12 Revamped record cabinet

Small cabinets like this can be picked up very cheaply. Originally used for storing records, the dividers inside work a treat for hallway shoe and bag storage. The original 1960s feel has been retained through the use of vibrant pink Formica to cover the cabinet top and doors.

creative kitchens

Until very recently it was virtually impossible to make over a kitchen successfully. Now, however, there are some amazing products available that work really well: cupboard paints that can cover melamine, slide-on transfers for tiles that don't necessarily feature 'olde worlde' scenes, water-based speciality paints such as magnet wall paint (applied under any other paint to produce a magnetic surface) and chalkboard paint which is great for providing a place in the family kitchen where children are actually allowed to draw on the walls! If you want a change of style, it really can take very little time to transform a plain, drab kitchen into a warm and inviting space with accents of colour. Traditionally the heart of the home, your kitchen can be a place where you spend a lot of time. Homely touches such as an eclectic set of painted chairs or a jaunty window blind can warm up a cool stainless steel space without losing you one iota of style.

pretty pastel chairs

Q How can I make over an old set of kitchen chairs? I love the shape but they just look dowdy. I have a bright and airy kitchen and like a touch of retro styling.

A Give your chairs a facelift with bright pastel paint and pretty new seat pads made from vintage teatowels. 'Furniture' or 'multi-surface' paints are the products to look out for, and water-based types will be quick-drying as well. Choose colours that are muted brights, like the colours you would find in 1950s textiles.

using paint

Old or new wooden chairs are easy to find and relatively inexpensive. Painting transforms them completely and can be a great design 'tool'. A uniform set of chairs can be livened up with a mix of toning colours – different several shades of green, for example. Conversely, an eclectic collection of wooden chairs can successfully be united by painting them all the same colour.

Painted furniture is very much back in fashion, and if you have a steady hand you could try painting chairs with simple Scandinavian-style designs. Adding a very fine-painted line in a dark tone to a chair back, following the contours of the chair, looks classically beautiful.

skill level
confident

colour palette
pastels

time taken
1 day

you will need

- Kitchen chairs (preferably that don't need stripping – you will need more time if they do)
- Medium-grade sandpaper
- Wire wool
- White spirit
- Multi-purpose primer
- 75 ml (1 quart) water-based furniture or multi-surface paint per chair
- Selection of teatowels – vintage, or new but traditional style. You will need 2 teatowels or 1 m (1¼ yd) other fabric, 145 cm (60 in) wide, per chair
- Approximately 2 m (2¼ yd) wadding (batting)
- 4 m (4½ yd) piping cord

tools

- 5 cm (2 in) paintbrush
- Scissors
- Graph or pattern-cutting paper and pencil
- Fabric scissors
- Pins
- Medium-gauge sewing needle
- Sewing machine (not essential, but quicker)
- Knitting needle

transforming the chairs

1 To prepare the chairs, sand lightly and then rub over them with wire wool to achieve a really smooth surface. Finally, wipe down with white spirit on a soft cloth, ready for the next step.

2 Even if the instructions for the paint you are using for your final finish say that it doesn't need a primer, it is still worth applying a coat. It's difficult to know exactly what is already on the surface of an old chair, and if you don't prime you may eventually find brown marks seeping through the paint finish.

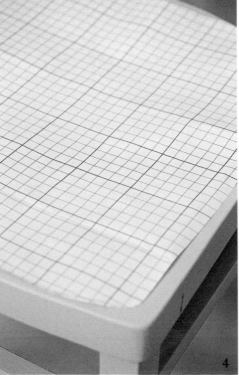

3 Apply two coats of your chosen colour, allowing the paint to dry thoroughly between coats. It helps to paint the underside of the chair first, as it can be tricky painting those hard-to-reach areas when the chair is upright.

4 Using graph or pattern-cutting paper, make a template for your seat pads. Measure the seat and draw the shape onto the paper – the ready-printed squares will help you. Then lay the paper pattern onto the chair and trim if necessary. Cut out one of these shapes from each of your teatowels or fabric lengths, adding a 2 cm (¾ in) seam allowance all round.

5 Cut out the wadding (batting) using the same template but without the seam allowance and pin centrally to the wrong side of one of the seat-pad sections. Machine or hand stitch into place with a line of stitching around the outside edge.

6 Make a long strip from your teatowel or fabric scraps – if you are using teatowels, you will probably have to join several pieces. The piping will look neater if you cut the fabric on the bias. To do this, spread out the fabric and cut 5 cm (2 in) strips diagonally across. Stitch them together to form the long strip. Place the piping cord in the middle of the strip on the wrong side and fold over the fabric, trapping the piping within. Pin to hold in place. With right sides together, pin the covered piping to the other seat-pad fabric piece (without the wadding/batting) at the edge and stitch into place. Remove all the pins. With right sides facing, pin the piped seat-pad section to the wadded section. Stitch together all round, leaving a 10 cm (4 in) gap. Turn the seat pad the right way out through the gap and neatly hand stitch the gap closed.

quick tip

Your chairs will look fantastic in the kitchen teamed with a plain wooden table or, best of all, a 1950s retro-style one topped with a pastel-coloured laminate. Although this effect is wonderful for chairs, do not be tempted into painting a table in the same way: you should not paint any surface where food preparation may take place, as the finish would not be hardwearing enough to withstand the use of knives or other utensils.

7 For each seat pad, make two fabric ties to tie the pad to the chair. Cut a strip of teatowel or fabric 30 cm (12 in) long and 5 cm (2 in) wide. With right sides together, fold it in half lengthways, pin and stitch along the long edges and one of the short edges, leaving the other short edge free. Turn the tie the right way out by pushing the short stitched end through the tube with a knitting needle. Press, then pin the ties onto the seat pad, placing it on the chair to find the correct position. Stitch into place.

new doors for old cupboards

Q My kitchen cupboards are perfectly serviceable, but I'm bored with them! How can I give them a whole new look without it costing the earth?

A Simply repainting kitchen cabinets can make a world of difference. You can also transform flat doors into Shaker style by adding a simple frame made from MDF (fibreboard). Add the moulding, then paint with cupboard makeover paint – using a brush for that 'handmade kitchen' look.

quick kitchen fixes

A kitchen is one of the most costly rooms to renovate. Luckily, there is now a wide range of products available to help you do just that. Dowdy tiles can make a kitchen gloomy, so why not invest in a few packs of 'tile transfers'? Simply soak briefly in water and then slide the transfer onto a dampened wall tile for a fantastic effect. You can also buy paint that is applied directly onto the wall tiles with no need for a separate primer. To achieve a successful look with tile paint, it is important to apply it with a mini sponge roller – and remember to re-grout between the tiles with fresh white grouting.

skill level
experienced

colour palette
aqua

time taken
1 day at least

making the doors

1 Remove each door from its cupboard using a screwdriver and then remove the handle. Measure very precisely for the MDF (fibreboard) panels. The two panels on either side run from top to bottom and the other two from side to side between the two side panels. Take the panels to be cut to size professionally, as unless you are an expert it is just too difficult to cut them as precisely as you need in order to achieve an excellent finish. Attach the panels to the front of the cupboard door with panel pins and a small hammer.

2 Punch the panel pins further down in their holes using a nail punch or a larger nail, so that they are below the surface of the MDF (fibreboard). Fill in the tiny holes with wood filler, using a filler knife or scraper. Allow to dry and then sand gently until the surface feels perfectly smooth when you run your hand over it.

3

quick tip

Simply painting plain cupboards and changing the handles will give you a dramatic makeover. Why not go for broke and choose a really striking fire-engine red or bubblegum pink? If your room is light and sunny the cooler shades of aqua and blue will work well, but if you have a darker kitchen choose warmer colours such as yellow and terracotta for a successful scheme.

3 Paint the front of the door with two coats of cupboard makeover, melamine or multi-surface paint, allowing the paint to dry completely between coats. A well-loaded brush will give you a better finish. Replace the handle, using the original screw holes on the rear of the door as a guide. Allow to dry overnight before re-hanging the door. If the handles weren't fitted right through the door, or if you need to reposition them, wait until all the doors have been re-hung. This way, you can choose an exact spot on each door, measure and attach according to the style of handle.

one shelf, three ways

Q **Can open kitchen shelving work in any space?**

A Take one simple pine shelf kit, consisting of shelf and wall brackets, and transform it into as many different looks as you can think of. Here are just three ways of looking at it... why stop at only one?

skill level
easy

colour palette
white

time taken
1 hour

1. country style

A punched paper liner gives a pretty and practical effect, reminiscent of a traditional lace shelf edging.

transforming the shelf

1 Lay the shelf on top of the paper. The paper has to fit over the top of the shelf as well. Decide how deep you want the edging to be, then fold the paper back against the shelf to get a firm crease. Do the same on both sides – the other side is simply folded under to create a neat finish.

2 Use a tape measure to find the central point and mark it in pencil. This will ensure the pattern looks symmetrical. Remember to make any marks on the reverse side of the paper.

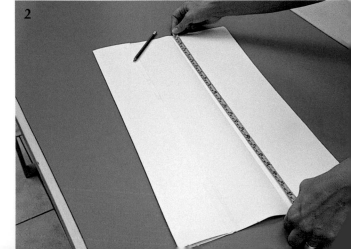

quick tip
You don't have to stick to white for this project. A brightly coloured paper will give a real Mexican fiesta flavour, and you can always change the colours and patterns with the seasons.

3 Using a saucer as a template and working from the marked centre point outwards, draw halfway around the edge of the saucer as many times as necessary to create a scalloped edge.

4 Scissors with a deckle-edged blade give a pretty finish and are available in many different styles. Cut around your marked scalloped edging.

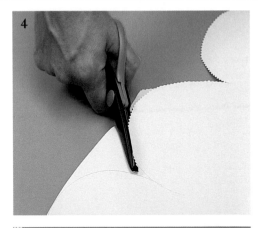

5 Have fun punching out your design with a selection of different motifs. Use a precise or a random design – the choice is yours. The punched-out paper 'confetti' is very pretty and can be used later for gift wrapping or table confetti. Fit the brackets to the shelf and then screw the shelf to the wall. A spirit level will help to ensure that it is straight. Then simply lay the liner over the shelf and admire your handiwork.

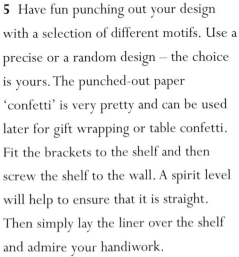

2. neutral and natural

Calico fabric and a set of baskets produce a soft, neutral effect — the little calico sacks are useful for keeping all those bits and pieces safely in one place.

making the shelf

1 Cut out a calico strip measuring approximately 40 x 25 cm (16 x 10 in). Fold in half widthways with right sides facing and machine or hand stitch up the longer sides, creating a long sack shape. Turn over a deep hem at the open end and stitch in place. Turn the bag the right way out. Fold out another hem to sit on the outside of the bag and stitch into place with a contrasting thread colour.

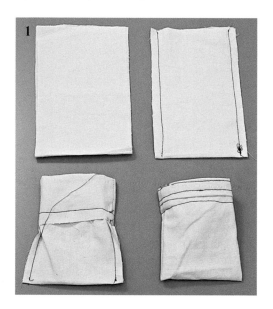

2 Using a scalpel blade, carefully make a small hole in one top edge of the bag. Punch an eyelet through it using an eyelet punch. Thread a 15-cm (6-in) length of string through the eyelet to form a simple handle. String is a good choice as it can be laundered easily along with the calico.

quick tip

The little bags can also be made in patterned fabrics – gingham and stripes work particularly well. You can also make other kitchen accessories in matching fabric. One of my favourites is a carrier bag 'sausage': simply make a tube of fabric with elasticized closures at each end and add a ribbon with which to hang it up. You will be amazed how many carrier bags you can stuff into the 'sausage', making recycling a tidy affair.

3 Sand the shelf lightly, then paint the woodwash directly onto the wood. It produces a lovely bleached effect that still shows the grain of the wood. You don't have to use any further finish.

4 Measure out positions for the little calico sacks (remember to allow for the shelf brackets) and mark with a pencil, then screw the cup hooks directly into the wood of the shelf at the marked points. Fit the brackets to the shelf and then screw the shelf to the wall. A spirit level will help to ensure that it is straight.

skill level
confident

colour palette
silver

time taken
3 hours

you will need

- Pine shelf kit
- Plastic dust sheet
- 1 can of silver spray paint
- 3 small jars, with lids that will accept screws (metal is good, plastic may shatter)
- Screws

tools

- Small hole punch or bradawl and hammer
- Cutting mat
- Tape measure and pencil
- Screwdriver
- Spirit level

3. contemporary styling

Silver metallic spray paint gives a modern touch to the shelf, while small jars attached to the underside are perfect for often-used spices such a salt and pepper.

making the shelf

1 Protect your working surface with a plastic dust sheet, then spray the shelf and brackets with silver metallic paint. There is no need to prime beforehand. It will take at least two coats to get a good silver effect.

2 Punch a small hole in each of the jar lids using a hole punch or a bradawl and hammer. Use a cutting mat to protect your working surface.

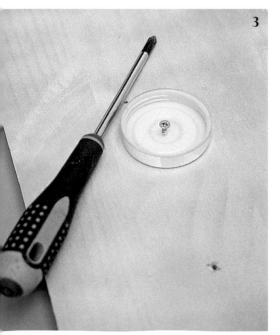

3 Measure the positions for the jars and mark with a pencil, remembering to allow for the shelf brackets, then screw the lids firmly into place. Fit the brackets to the shelf and then screw the shelf to the wall. A spirit level will help to ensure that it is straight.

quick tip

This shelf would also be excellent in a home office space, using the containers for paper clips, rubber bands and drawing pins, for example.

vibrant vertical blinds

Q **I have some vertical blinds for my kitchen door, but I find the plain white slats a little uninspiring, especially in the summer months. I'd love to ring the changes now and again with some different colours.**

A Make your own replacement slats. Designer options for vertical blinds are available but tend to be costly. Fabric stiffener spray will turn candy-coloured plain glazed cotton into the ideal fabric for a vertical blind.

using fabric stiffener

Once you discover how easy fabric stiffener is to use, you will be unstoppable! You could make a whole series of vertical slats to change with the seasons. Natural tones of linen would work very well, and for a really funky 'boho' effect try treating heavier cotton lace and net fabrics with the spray – beautiful for a festive season. You can, of course, use the stiffener to make regular blinds for your windows from virtually any fabric, although cotton will give the best results for long-term use. You can also refresh existing blinds if they are looking a bit limp.

you will need

- Vertical blind set, to fit your door or window
- Approximately 2 m (2¼ yd) of each of your chosen fabrics – quantities may vary depending on the door or window size, so base the measurement on the length of the drop
- Matching sewing threads
- 1 pack of spray-on fabric stiffener
- Several lengths of scrap wallpaper – *not* ready-pasted

tools

- Pins
- Fabric scissors
- Medium-gauge sewing needle
- Sewing machine (not essential, but quicker)
- Tape measure and pencil

skill level
easy

colour palette
ice-cream pastels

time taken
6 hours

making the blinds

1 Use one of the existing slats as a pattern guide to cut out your replacement slats. Pin it onto the fabric and cut out around it – cut out as many as you want in each colour, plus a few extras in case of any mistakes later (see step 3). Don't worry too much about length: as long as you allow plenty of fabric, you can adjust to fit at a later stage. There is no need for a seam allowance either, as the fabric stiffener also acts as a seal, preventing any fraying around the edges of the fabric slats.

2 The weights of a vertical blind help it to hang correctly and are held in a large hem at the bottom of each fabric slat. Again using the original slat as a guide to depth, machine or hand stitch the hem on each new slat.

3

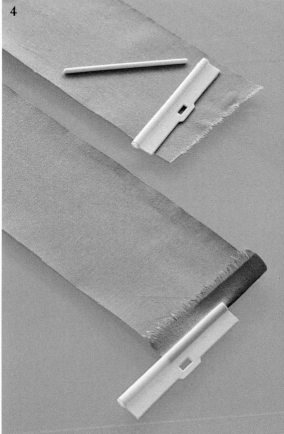

4

3 The fabric stiffener comes ready-mixed in a handy spray. Surplus wallpaper makes an ideal base on which to work. Soak the fabric slats thoroughly with the spray. This is where you may need a few spare slats on which to practise your technique: the result can be blotchy if you use too little or too much spray, so carry out a trial run or two. Have another couple of lengths of wallpaper ready onto which to transfer the drying slats – move them to another paper length when they are half-dry to prevent them sticking. The slats may look a little wrinkled as they dry, but this disappears once they are totally dry.

4 Before you hang the blinds you will need to set the length. There is a clever bar and slot method on most blinds. Measure the fabric slat to the required length, mark with a pencil and fold along the mark. Place the bar inside the fold and then slot into the carrying mechanism. For a fun look, vary the lengths and use a mix of candy colours.

découpage mirror

Q I have a plain wooden-framed mirror that I'd really like to cover with some kind of pattern, but I'm not an artist. Can I cover the frame with something?

A Découpage is a good solution. This mirror was inspired by some fabulous papier mâché bowls covered with sardine can labels that I saw on a trip to Cape Town, South Africa.

you will need

- Mirror with wooden baseboard or frame (not too wide)
- Selection of can labels
- Fine-grade sandpaper
- PVA adhesive
- Small can of water-based matt varnish

tools

- Scalpel blade or craft knife
- Scissors
- Medium-sized old paintbrush

decorating mirrors

Just painting a simple frame can give a room a new look. Many of the other techniques described in this book can be used on a mirror frame. Gilding, distressing and handpainting a design would all work extremely well, and would also be good test pieces to see if you enjoy a particular technique. And it doesn't only have to be the frame, as you can see with the Skeleton Leaves Mirror on page 40. Decorating the mirror surface is effective and fun – glass paints, stickers and frostings are all good resources for glass and mirror decorating.

skill level
confident

colour palette
red/black

time taken
8 hours

decorating the mirror

1 Unless you are a sardine aficionado, you may find tomato (or other vegetable) can labels easier to stomach! As a guide, you will need approximately 15 labels for a 60 x 30 cm (24 x 12 in) mirror with a frame 5 cm (2 in) wide. Remove the labels from the cans using a scalpel blade or craft knife. Work carefully, slicing the back of the label in two and peeling it away from the can. The blade is useful for easing away any stubborn areas. Once the labels have been removed, use scissors to trim them neatly and cut away any uninteresting text or barcodes.

1

2 Sand the mirror frame to ensure that the adhesive will get a good grip – it won't work so well if the surface is shiny. Coat the frame with a medium layer of PVA adhesive and stick on the labels in a random pattern. Layer them where necessary, using more adhesive when you do so. You are aiming for a random effect with none of the original wooden surface showing through.

2

3

3 Using an old paintbrush, apply as many coats of water-based matt varnish as you have patience for. Running your finger over the joins and pressing down on the wet varnish as you go will improve the overall finish (latex gloves are particularly useful here).

quick tip

Once you get the knack of successful découpage you can choose from many different projects. Old-fashioned reproduction 'scraps' can be found in craft shops and are lovely for smaller pieces. Try more unusual ideas such as old sheet music, foreign newsprint, or even photocopy your holiday snaps in black and white to give them a 'retro' feel.

creative kitchens gallery

1 Chunky bead tablecloth weights

Extra tables can be constructed from a sheet of MDF (fibreboard) and a pair of trestles, and hidden under a cloth. Here, a brightly patterned oilcloth is perfect for a children's party, with tablecloth weights made from curtain clips, wire and chunky beads and hung from the corners of the tablecloth.

2 Blank canvas papercloth

Don't leave all the fun to the youngsters! Cover a quick-fix trestle table with a papercloth and provide a jar of wax crayons and a paper cloth for budding artists of all ages.

3 Go outside

Roof slates make an interesting outdoor table surface. If you want to make this a permanent feature, choose marine ply or water-retardant MDF (fibreboard).

4 Retro-style café curtain

Scan images from old recipe books and print them onto fabric transfer paper. Iron onto plain white fabric and then stitch onto a bright gingham café-style curtain.

5 Plastic-strip curtain

Plastic-strip door curtains cut down to café-style length add a touch of bright colour to a modern kitchen.

6 Wooden cutlery box

To make a cutlery storage box, add a carrying handle made from rope to a plain wooden letter rack. A coat of water-based matt varnish will keep it looking pristine.

7 Decorative pulls

Even though the blind operates with a side winding mechanism, a decorative pull will add a finishing touch. Buttons and buckles make an unusual and stylish alternative.

8 Ribbon trim

A split-and-weave effect with ribbon provides a pretty border to a plain blind. Finish by stitching on a neat length of braiding.

9 Flower stamp border

A floral stamp motif is another way of adding a decorative touch to a plain white blind.

10 Chalkboard

Use magnetic paint under chalkboard paint to create a useful memo board.

11 Easy view

Remove the doors altogether and replace with storage baskets for everyday items or box files to tidy loose recipes.

12 French bread box

These wooden boxes for storing French bread are extremely practical and add a rustic touch to a country-style kitchen. This one had seen better days, so was made over with a crackle-glaze effect. Water-based versions are now available and work well, but you will need to finish with an oil-based varnish.

beautiful bedrooms

Whatever your personal style, you will find plenty of scope for bedroom facelifts here. Screens are a lovely idea in a bedroom — choose from soft florals for a traditional boudoir look or boldly printed contemporary shapes for an ultra-modern room. Use them to divide a room or to disguise storage.

Take a second look at that tired old chest of drawers or bedside table and see if a fresh approach can give it a new lease of life: it's amazing what a simple coat of paint can do.

Hand-me-down pieces of Lloyd Loom furniture can be restyled to suit your sanctuary, and if you fancy a glittery bedhead, go right ahead! Unusual and delicate pieces can find the perfect home in a bedroom — a pretty caned chair is a satisfying project and sure to become a future heirloom.

A headboard is often the focal point of a bedroom and a large-scale version can really 'finish' a room. Create a modern patchwork (as on page 94) or go for one dramatic statement fabric.

Lloyd Loom chair

Q **This chair has a charming style but needs to fit into a more contemporary space. Where do I start?**

A The woodwork can be lifted with a waxed lime effect that works well with celadon colour paint used on the woven body of the chair. New upholstery and a cute matching bag complete the revamp. The chair is simple in shape so will take a more contemporary theme.

finding Lloyd Loom

Lloyd Loom furniture is actually made from twisted paper partly reinforced with steel wire, not wicker as you might think at first glance. Invented in 1907, it is still being made today. Pieces from the 1930s to the 1950s are still easy to find and make great facelift projects. Try flea markets, small ads in local papers, thrift stores and house clearance sales – all good general sources of facelift material. Alternatively, you may find that an elderly relative has one or two items of Lloyd Loom lurking in the attic. The treatment shown here would also work well with wicker or cane pieces, but be sure to sand them lightly before painting.

skill level
confident

colour palette
celadon

time taken
8 hours

you will need

- Lloyd Loom chair
- Medium-grade sandpaper
- Sugar soap
- 1 litre (2 quarts) liquid-wax liming fluid
- 1 litre (2 quarts) multi-surface or furniture paint
- Approximately 0.5 m (¾ yd) calico, wide enough to cover the seat (if required)
- Approximately 0.5 m (¾ yd) decorative fabric, wide enough to cover the seat
- Matching sewing thread

tools

- Stiff brush
- Medium-sized old paintbrush
- Pliers
- Fabric scissors
- Staple gun and staples

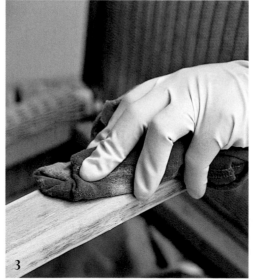

2 This step uses a brush-on, liquid-wax liming fluid. The real thing involves a scary number of chemicals and procedures, so a product like this is fantastic for a furniture facelift. Simply apply the wax using an old paintbrush and allow to dry.

transforming the chair

1 Sand the woodwork. Stripping was unnecessary on this piece: to decide whether or not you need to strip your chair, carry out a test sand on a small area to check if this will be enough to achieve a matt surface. Using a stiff brush, work your way over the whole chair to remove all dust and debris. Wash down with sugar soap to remove any greasy residue that may have accumulated over time.

3 Buff down the dried wax with a soft, clean rag and the limed effect will appear before your eyes. The wax also provides a protective finish, so no further sealant is required to the wood.

4 Multi-surface paint can be used on virtually any surface and is formulated to be especially flexible, making it ideal for Lloyd Loom style or wicker furniture. Use an old paintbrush and work the paint really well into the surface.

6 Using the seat as a template, cut out the required shape from decorative fabric. Allow plenty of extra all round for ease of working, including enough to turn over and give a neat edge underneath.

7 Staple the fabric neatly to the underside of the seat pad, stretching and checking that the fabric is smooth over the seat surface as you go.

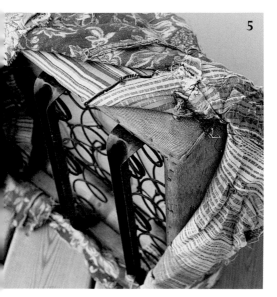

5 If the original seat-pad cover is in reasonable condition, it's worth leaving it as a base from which to work. Otherwise, remove the old cover, using pliers to pull out any stubborn tacks or staples. Re-cover with calico in the same way as for the main seat fabric – see step 7.

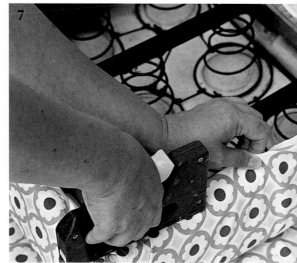

quick tip

Why not run up a little matching bag with any left-over fabric scraps? All you need are two rectangles of fabric each 20 x 15 cm (8 x 6 in) to make the bag, and two strips each 20 x 10 cm (8 x 4 in) for the handles. With right sides facing, machine or hand stitch the bag pieces together around three sides, leaving one of the shorter edges open. To make the handles, fold the strips in half lengthways with right sides facing and stitch along the long edge. Turn inside out. Pin the handles to the inside edge of the bag and stitch in place.

Lloyd Loom linen basket

Q I've found a sweet little laundry basket that has seen one makeover too many! I'd like to give it a more sophisticated look for a guest bedroom.

A You can't fail with white. A simple spray job for the basket, a scrap of silk and some interesting trim make this sorry old basket look very smart indeed.

look out for Lloyd Loom

Lloyd Loom furniture was manufactured in many different styles that work especially well in bedrooms. Easy to find are linen baskets, ottomans and blanket boxes, but keep an eye out for more interesting pieces such as occasional tables, kidney-shaped dressing tables and even wall-mounted mirrors with Lloyd Loom frames. As you can see from the linen basket shown here, these pieces were probably among the first types of furniture to be given a facelift.

you will need

- Lloyd Loom linen basket
- 0.5 m (¾ yd) wadding (batting), wide enough to cover the lid
- 0.5 m (¾ yd) calico, wide enough to cover the lid (optional)
- 0.5 m (¾ yd) plaid silk fabric, wide enough to cover the lid
- 1 m (1¼ yd) fringe trim
- Matching sewing thread
- 2 cans of white matt spray paint
- Plastic dust sheets

tools

- Fabric scissors
- Staple gun and staples
- Curved upholstery or repair needle

skill level
easy

colour palette
white/coffee/black

time taken
5 hours

transforming the linen basket

1 Sometimes furniture facelifts can provide a fascinating glimpse into the past of your chosen piece. Here you can see decades of different fabrics as new covers have simply been placed one on top of another. To get a neat new look, I removed the lid from the box and then removed all the layers of the lid.

2 The lid wasn't originally upholstered, but a pad made from wadding (batting) will improve the overall smartness of the piece. Wadding can also be used to replace any worn-out foam or quilting, sometimes used for seat pads like this. Use the seat as a template to cut out a piece of wadding large enough to tuck just under the lid. Keep it snug, as it is quite stretchy and if fitted loosely may look lumpy. To keep the inside neat, staple the waddling (batting) to the inside rim of the lid, not the underside.

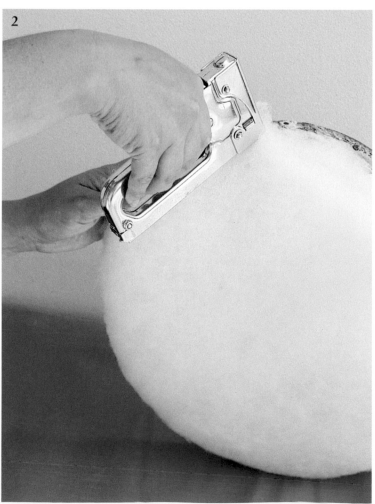

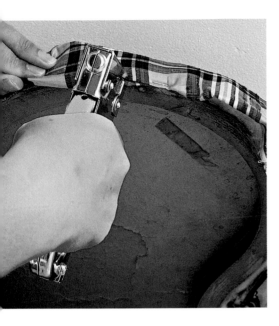

5 Spray paint gives a great effect to the finished linen basket, but you must use it in a well-ventilated space with lots of dust sheets. To achieve a good finish, begin and end each spray away from the basket. Sweep from side to side, and be sure to finish the last sweep off the basket. Apply as many coats as necessary to cover the original paint, turning the basket upside down for the final coat to ensure that the paint gets into every spot. When it's completely dry, re-attach the lid.

3 If you are using a fine fabric like the silk shown here, it helps to make an interlining from calico. Use the seat as a template to cut a piece of calico that is large enough to tuck well under the lid. Staple in place in the same way as for the wadding (batting), keeping everything as neat as you can. Repeat this process for the final fabric cover.

4 Hand stitch the trim all around the lid, attaching it to the fabric. It is better to do this with the lid resting on the box as it will be when fitted, to ensure that the trim is positioned correctly. A curved upholstery or repair needle is a real help here. It will be neater if you start attaching the trim at the back of the seat.

quick tip

Padding the seat gives a more finished look but if you are using a thicker fabric anyway, you could dispense with the wadding (batting). Thicker fabrics that will work well are velvet, tweed or even fluffy fake fur for a really fun look.

mirrored dressing table

Q I just love the mirrored Art Deco style furniture, but it's very expensive. Is this easy to do yourself?

A If you choose a simple piece of furniture to start with and measure well, then it is very easy! Having a suitable (that is, safe thickness) mirror cut to size is quite pricey, but you can still make yourself a mirrored dressing table for half the cost of buying one ready-made.

you will need

- Suitable table
- Mirror, cut to size by a glazier
- Mirror adhesive (available from glaziers and specialist suppliers)
- Fine-grade sandpaper

tools

- Tape measure

versatile mirror

Mirror is a wonderful material. You can use webbing-backed mirror mosaic sheets for all kinds of facelifts including frames, wall panels, lining the backs of cupboards and covering cylinder vases. If you aren't superstitious, you can make your own mosaic by smashing old mirrors or mirror tiles into small pieces and using with dual-purpose tile adhesive/grout to create mirrored masterpieces. Old mirrors made with traditional 'silvering' techniques grow old very gracefully and the distressed-looking glass can become a decorative element in its own right. Use it as a display, mounting photographs or pictures directly onto the glass mirror surface.

skill level
confident

colour palette
natural

time taken
2 hours

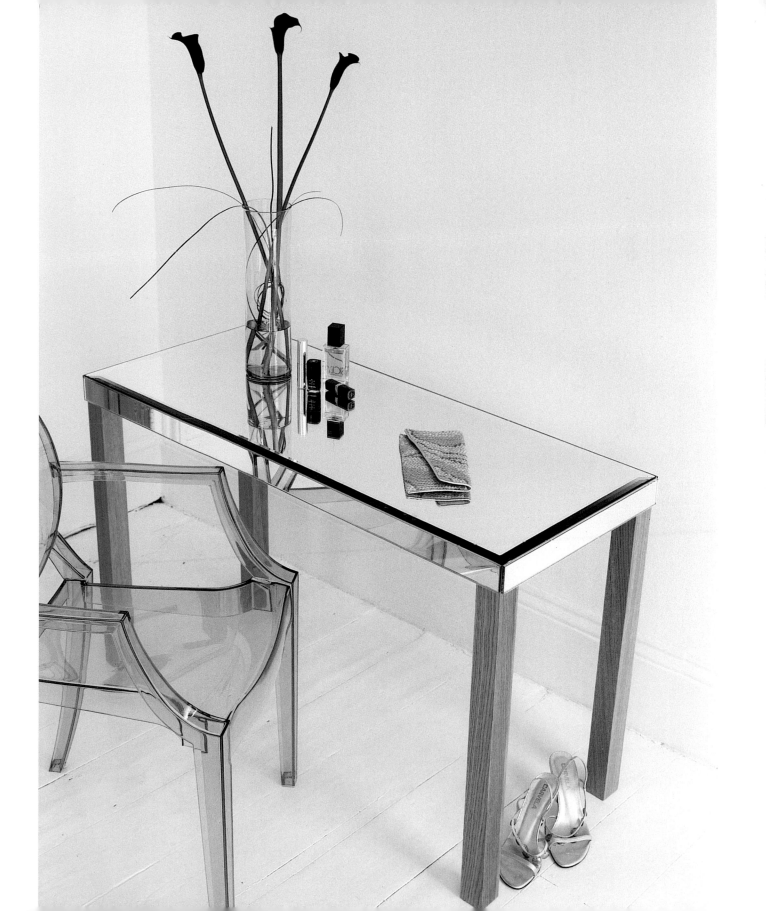

making the dressing table

1 This is the most important step for this project and you must get it right. It pays to measure once, twice, and then once more for luck! You need to measure the width and length of the tabletop, and depth and length of the side pieces (five pieces in all). Remember to allow for some overlap if you don't want to see the original finish peeking through at the corners. Remove the legs of the table and place the top on a secure, flat surface to make it easier to work with.

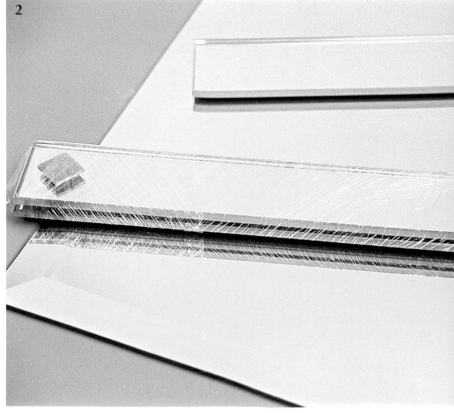

2 Have all the mirror pieces cut to size. Tell your glazier what you are planning and he will ensure that the mirror is of the correct thickness – if it is too thin, it may shatter easily. The top surface will look gorgeous with a bevelled edge, but the sides will be too narrow to allow for this. Make sure the glazier smoothes off all the edges.

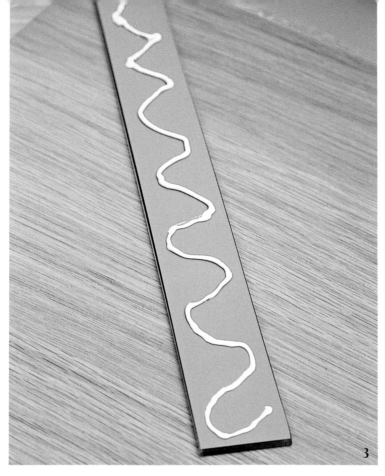

3 Sand the surface of the table side pieces lightly. This will ensure that the adhesive works at maximum efficiency – it won't work quite as well on a shiny surface. Check again that the tabletop is perfectly level, otherwise the mirror pieces may slip. Apply the adhesive liberally to the mirror pieces and glue them into place.

4 Apply the adhesive liberally and evenly to the tabletop surface, then fit the tabletop mirror section. Another pair of hands may be necessary, as the mirror will be fairly heavy. Leave to dry overnight before reassembling the table.

quick tip

Other pieces traditionally covered with mirror glass are chests of drawers and wardrobes. A chest of drawers will look amazing if covered completely with glass, Hollywood starlet style, but will appear understated and gorgeous if you just face the drawers with mirror. Do bear in mind that the more mirror you add to a piece, the heavier it will become.

Oriental screen

Q I love the idea of a folding screen for my bedroom but want something contemporary to fit my space. What can you suggest?

A Give a simple three-fold screen a contemporary facelift using traditional techniques: one side with lush silver leaf and the other painted with Mandarin-red gloss. A decorative poppy appliqué adds a finishing touch and creates a stunning oriental-inspired piece that looks at home in a modern setting.

making screens

'Blanks' such as this screen make terrific weekend projects: more expensive than junk-store treasures, but all ready and waiting for you to personalize without the need for stripping and sanding. Alternatively, you can make your own MDF (fibreboard) screen by getting the panels cut to size at a timber yard and then buying 'piano hinges' from a DIY store. These long hinges fold both ways, allowing the screen to be very flexible.

If the gilding effect shown here looks a little daunting, you can try other beautiful metallic effects such as a glitter top coat or pearlescent finish.

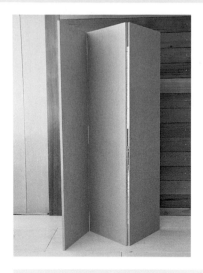

skill level
experienced

colour palette
red/silver

time taken
1½ days

you will need

- 3-fold 'blank' screen (usually made from MDF/fibreboard)
- 1 litre (2 quarts) multi-purpose primer
- 1 litre (2 quarts) Mandarin-red non-drip gloss paint
- 1 litre (2 quarts) size (glue used for gilding, available from art stores and specialist suppliers)
- Books of silver or aluminium leaf – take the measurements to your art store and they will ensure you buy the correct quantity (this screen has 3 panels each 150 x 50 cm (60 x 20 in) and used 6 books of aluminium leaf)
- Selection pack of patterned origami paper or wrapping paper
- Small can of spray-mount adhesive
- Plastic dust sheet
- 1 litre (2 quarts) oil-based gloss varnish
- Approximately 10 m (11 yd) braid, same width as the thickness of the screen panels

tools

- Medium-sized old paintbrush
- Good quality 'non-shedding' 5 cm (2 in) paintbrush
- Tracing paper and pencil
- Scissors
- Glue gun

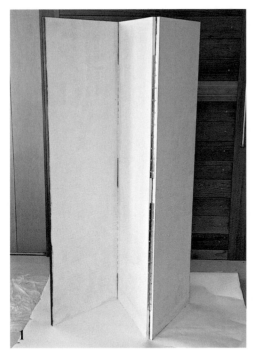

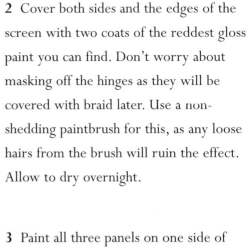

2 Cover both sides and the edges of the screen with two coats of the reddest gloss paint you can find. Don't worry about masking off the hinges as they will be covered with braid later. Use a non-shedding paintbrush for this, as any loose hairs from the brush will ruin the effect. Allow to dry overnight.

making the screen

1 Apply primer to the screen. Even on a new piece of wood or MDF (fibreboard), this is an essential step to achieving the perfect finish. Use an old paintbrush for this and work on a plastic dust sheet.

3 Paint all three panels on one side of the screen with size, using an old paintbrush. Don't worry that it will all dry before you have finished, as it stays live for some time. The size looks like white PVA adhesive when it is first applied and dries clear. At this point it is ready to be gilded.

4 The silver or aluminium leaf comes as a series of leaves backed with transfer papers, presented in a little book to keep them safe as they are very fragile. Carefully remove each leaf from the book as required.

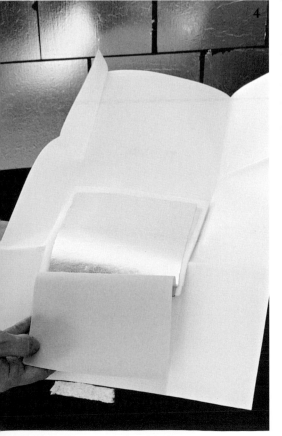

5 Apply the leaf transfer face down onto the screen and rub gently with your finger. Be bold, and don't worry too much about being precise. A little randomness actually enhances the effect.

6 Gently peel away the backing paper. Don't worry if some bits of leaf flake or pull away, as this distressing adds to the charm of the gilded effect.

quick tip

As an alternative to the silver leaf you could use silver spray paint. The finished look won't be quite as awe-inspiring, but will still be effective. Protect your working area with a plastic dust sheet. Decide which part of the screen to work on first and then cover the rest with newspaper – masking tape will keep it secure. Use masking tape to mark out sections for spraying and then cover the areas not to be sprayed with more newspaper. Build up the layers of paint gradually by spraying on fine coats until you are happy with the effect. When the paint is dry, remove the tape very carefully so as not to peel off any paint with it. Repeat with the other sections of the screen.

7 When the squares of silver or aluminium leaf are all in place, rub over with a soft cloth – a circular motion produces the best effect. Be very gentle as you don't want to remove any of the gilding.

8 Trace the template provided onto tracing paper and use this to cut out one of each of the poppy seedheads and one flower from origami paper or wrapping paper. Cut out some freehand stem sections as well – make them slightly curvy for a more natural effect.

9 Using spray-mount adhesive, attach the poppies to the centre panel of the plain red side. Using the old paintbrush, paint the whole screen with a layer of oil-based gloss varnish: water-based won't work well on the gilding. Finish by attaching braid to the edges of the panels using a glue gun, covering the hinges as you go.

stencil templates

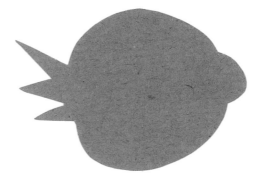

finished stencil on screen

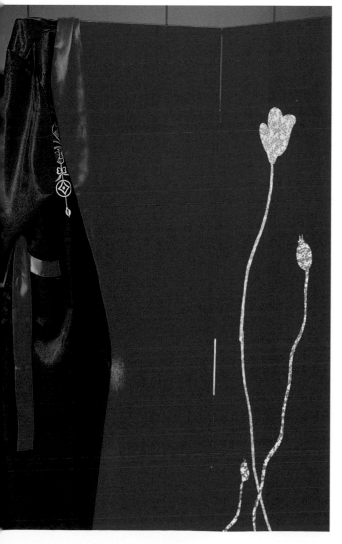

pretty patchwork headboard

Q I recently stayed in a hotel with a gorgeous fabric headboard, which was perfectly supportive for reading and watching TV but soft and pretty, too. How can I make one for myself?

A This classic headboard will brighten up any bed. The fabrics you choose govern the mood, so make sure you're really happy with the combination before you start. Gingham and swirls are used here, but it works well with any fabrics in complementary tones.

choosing your fabric

Select different fabrics that have a mix of textures but are a similar shade. You may be inspired by a treasured scrap of vintage silk or perhaps a piece of expensive fabric. You don't need to cover the whole board, but it looks more finished if you do. Just use plainer pieces for areas under the bed that won't be seen easily.

To calculate how much fabric you need, work out the square footage of your board. Divide the width evenly into at least five sections to give you the width of each finished patch. Cut your fabrics to this width, plus 2 cm (¾ in) for the seam allowance. You can use two different heights for added variation if you like. Seven different fabrics were used here.

you will need

- Piece of chipboard, cut to the bed width plus 50 cm (20 in) and as high as you like
- 5 cm (2 in) thick wadding (batting), cut to the size of the chipboard plus 8–10 cm (3–4 in) overlap all round
- Fabric pieces (see left), approximately 3 m (3½ yd) in total
- Tacking thread
- Sewing thread to tone with the fabric pieces
- 8 self-cover buttons
- 8 small buttons for fixing
- Mirror-hanging kit

tools

- Tape measure
- Fabric scissors
- Electric or hand drill with 3 mm (⅛ in) drill bit
- Staple gun and staples
- Pins
- 8 medium-gauge sewing needle
- Sewing machine (not essential, but quicker)

skill level
confident

colour palette
blues/lilacs

time taken
4 hours

making the headboard

1 Drill a line of 3 mm (⅛ in) holes in the chipboard, halfway between where the pillows end and the top of the board. Make the holes around 20 cm (8 in) apart. These will be used for attaching buttons later.

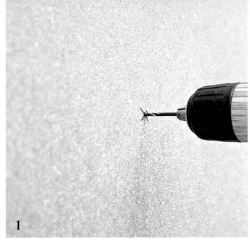

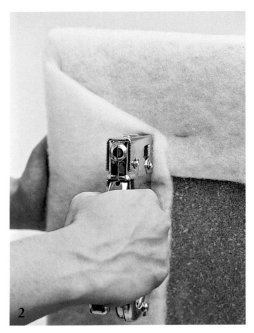

2 Cover the board with a layer of wadding (batting), allowing an overlap of 8–10 cm (3–4 in) of wadding around each edge. Fold the wadding over the back of the board, keeping the corners as flat as possible, and staple it to the back.

3 Lay the board on the floor and position your fabric pieces. Play around until you are happy with the effect.

4 Pin and tack the pieces together to form vertical strips, then machine or hand stitch them firmly into place.

5 Pin and tack, then stitch the strips together to form the patchwork. Check the size by laying it over the chipboard.

6

6 Fold the patchwork over the board and attach it in the same way as the wadding (batting). For best results, pin then staple.

7 Cover the buttons with left-over fabric. Cut a circle of fabric 1.25 cm (½ in) bigger in diameter than the button top. Work a line of running stitch about 3 mm (⅛ in) from the edge of the circle. Place the button top in the centre of the fabric and pull the thread so that the stitches gather and pull the fabric tight around the button. Fasten off. Press the button into position. Create a quilted effect by threading cotton through the back of the holes in the board, looping it through the buttons, threading it back through the board again and securing using the smaller buttons.

quick tip

As in smart hotels, the board will look best wall mounted. You can do this using concealed mirror fixings or hangings, which attach to both the headboard and the wall. If you attach the headboard to the bed, to allow for repositioning the bed around the room, you will need to pre-drill holes in the chipboard that correspond to the fixtures on your bed. This option is not recommended if you are going for a glamorously tall headboard.

7

re-caning a delicate chair

Q I couldn't resist this little chair at an auction. It's pretty but needs re-caning – is this something I can attempt myself? I'd also like to paint it but would still like it to look of its period.

A This pretty occasional chair is perfect for a bedroom. The cane seat is destroyed and the varnish finish drab. Painting and distressing gives a sophisticated finish and re-caning is a skill that is straight-forward and makes a very satisfying project.

traditional crafts

This project was fairly time-consuming to complete. However, instead of being frustrating it was very soothing to work on, and I can certainly see why basket-weaving skills are regarded as successful therapy! Although I am first in line when it comes to searching out new time-saving wonder products, it is also exciting to revisit some more traditional crafts. Woodworking, embroidery, quilting and weaving are other ever-popular and rewarding crafts, and there are generally courses available to help you learn more about your chosen hobby.

skill level
experienced

colour palette
cream/grey

time taken
2 days

you will need

- Suitable chair
- 1 can of spray-on paint-stripping mousse
- Methylated spirits
- Wire wool
- Fine- and medium-grade sandpapers
- 1 litre (2 quarts) multi-purpose primer
- 1 litre (2 quarts) taupe multi-surface or furniture paint
- 1 litre (2 quarts) pale grey-white multi-surface or furniture paint
- Approximately 24 golf tees
- 1 hank of no. 2 cane
- 1 hank of no. 4 cane
- 1 length of no. 6 cane

NOTE The cane I used was soft enough to work with as it was. However, you may need to soak each section of cane for about ten minutes before use to make it more pliable.

tools

- Paint scraper
- 2 cm (¾ in) paintbrush
- Craft knife
- Scissors

re-caning the chair

1 Remove the old cane and then strip down the varnish – the new mousse applications are good for applying paint stripper to wood. Follow the instructions for your product – I had to apply one coat, leave for ten minutes, apply another coat and leave for 20 minutes.

2 Using a paint scraper, gently ease away the old varnish. You will need to wear latex gloves for this task.

3 Use wire wool and methylated spirits to clean away any remaining varnish. Allow to dry, then rub down gently with fine-grade sandpaper.

4 Apply a coat of primer. This is an easy step to miss out, but if you do so the final finish may be spoiled by old residue oils seeping through and leaving unattractive brown marks. Apply an undercoat of a darker colour than the top coat, such as this taupe. Allow to dry completely.

quick tip

It is possible to purchase ready-woven cane panelling, but this isn't suitable for a hand-caned chair frame. What's the difference? If there is a groove with a rounded cane filet fitted into it holding the cane in place, this is cane panelling. If there is a line of holes drilled around the edge of the seat, this is a hand-caned frame.

5 Apply the top coat of paint – a grey-white was used here – and allow to dry completely. Then remove some of the top layer using medium-grade sandpaper, to show the darker colour underneath. This 'distressing' looks most effective when used on areas that naturally receive wear, such as the seat back, around the legs and any edges. Sand lightly all over with fine-grade sandpaper to achieve a smooth finish.

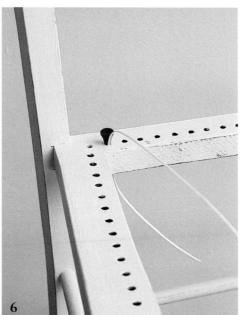

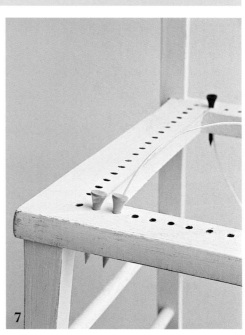

6 To begin the re-caning, insert one end of a length of no. 2 cane through the hole next to the corner hole at the back left-hand side of the chair seat. Make sure that the glossy side of the cane is facing up as it runs towards the front rail of the chair. Leave about 10 cm (4 in) of the cane projecting under the frame and hold it in place by pushing a golf tee into the same hole.

7 Keeping the glossy side up, take the end of the cane through the corresponding hole in the front rail, pulling it taut and securing with another tee. Push the end up through the next hole along the rail and secure with another tee.

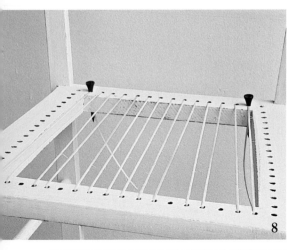

8 Continue as in step 7 all the way across the seat. You can move the tees along from hole to hole as you work. If, as in this case, there are more holes on the front rail than the back, simply miss out a few (evenly spaced) holes on the front rail. If you need to start a fresh section of cane, simply secure the end with a tee as in step 6 and continue.

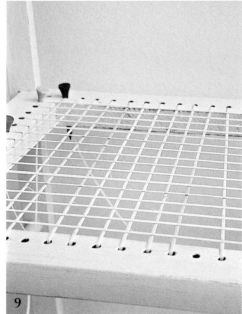

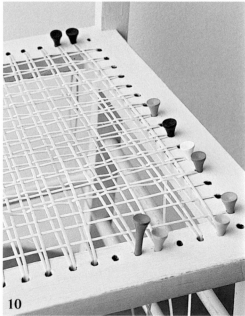

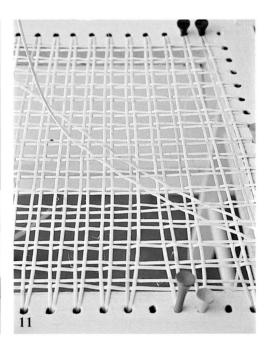

9 The next step, called the first weaving, is worked in the same way as the first setting but from side to side, with the cane (glossy side up) passing over the top of the first setting. Now repeat the first setting. Try to position the new cane slightly to one side of the original, as this will make the following steps easier to work.

10 For the second weaving, run the cane through your fingers. The snag-free way is the right way to pull. Otherwise the cane is liable to split the existing canes. Work as for the first weaving, but thread the cane under the first setting cane and over the second setting cane. Weave about six strokes before pulling the cane through, as this will keep it looking neat.

11 Change to no. 4 cane for the first diagonal. Peg into the back left-hand corner. Weave OVER the first pair of weavings, count down a row and UNDER the first pair of settings. Count down a row and continue until you reach the front rail. As before, there may be more holes on the front rail than the back. In this case, use some holes twice.

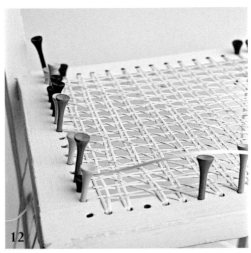

12 The second diagonal is the opposite of the first diagonal. Working from the back right-hand corner, you now need to pass UNDER the horizontals and OVER the verticals. By now you will probably have lots of tees holding ends in place.

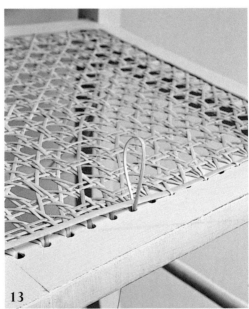

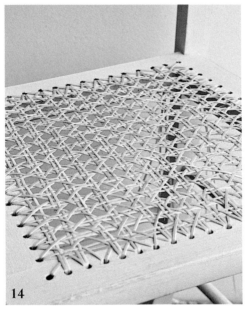

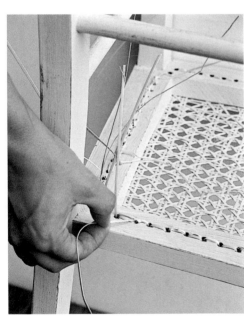

13 Remove the tees ready for the finishing process.

14 To finish the caning neatly with 'beading', lay a length of no. 6 cane over the holes around the rail. Run a length of no. 2 cane through a hole from underneath, over the no. 6 cane and back down through the same hole. Continue around the rail, using every hole in the same way.

15 Turn the chair upside down so that you can tie in the ends. Thread each loose end of cane under an adjacent loop once, then back and under itself. Trim neatly with scissors.

one table, two ways: 1. Toile de Jouy

Q **I am trying to create a soft, gentle look in my bedroom but it's proving difficult to find pretty patterned furniture. What do you suggest?**

A A simple fabric covering will soften and 'pretty up' a wooden bedside table, making it perfect for a gentle scheme.

alternative treatments

Although this type of table is usually varnished already, you can still paint them easily with multi-surface – just give the wood a light sanding first. Choosing the fabric for a project such as this will make the table look different every time. A pretty fabric such as this Toile will give a feminine feel whilst a heavy linen will do wonders for a softly modern bedroom. This is also a great way to use a piece of vintage fabric or remnants left from making your curtains.

skill level
easy

colour palette
monochrome

time taken
1 hour

making the cover

1 Measure the tabletop very accurately, then add 2 cm (¾ in) for a seam allowance all round. Mark out the measurements on your fabric with tailor's chalk and then cut out.

2 Cut out four more pieces of fabric for the table cover sides. These should be the same length as each of the sides of the top piece and approximately 30 cm (12 in) deep. Fold a 2 cm (¾ in) hem along one long and two shorter edges of each of the four side pieces.

3 Pin the unfinished edge of one side piece to the top piece – it won't fit edge to edge because you have used the seam allowance. Machine or hand stitch into place. Repeat with the other three side pieces. Press out all the seams.

4 Cut out eight pieces of fabric for the ties, each 5 x 30 cm (2 x 12 in). Fold one piece in half lengthways with right sides facing and pin in place, to create a long thin tube. Stitch across one short end and down the long side, leaving one short edge open. Turn the tube right side out and press. Repeat with the remaining seven pieces.

5 Pin one tie approximately 15 cm (6 in) down from the tabletop centrally on each short side of every side piece and stitch in place. Press out all the seams. Lay the cover over the table and tie each pair of corner ties with a pretty bow.

quick tip

The fabric you choose for this project will really set the scene. The Toile de Jouy fills the romantic brief. Gingham or checks will create a country style; a heavy, suede effect will suit contemporary spaces; and natural linen is perfect for a global-inspired theme.

2. Art Deco

Q A basic side table makes a roomy bedside table that is fine as it is – but how can I tie it into my Art Deco scheme?

A A marble-topped table would fit the bill perfectly but is an expensive option. Recreate that look by using vinyl floor tiles at a fraction of the cost.

you will need
- Plain wooden table
- 1 pack of 30 x 30 cm (12 x 12 in) self-adhesive vinyl floor tiles

tools
- Metal ruler and pencil
- Cutting mat
- Craft knife

contemporary styling

Simple, reasonably priced modern pieces are perfect subjects for facelift projects. It's not always easy to find vintage pieces that will work in your home and if you like contemporary style this will suit you very well. A simple flat-packed melamine wardrobe, for example, is easily transformed into a designer-style cupboard by using brightly coloured melamine/cupboard paints and masking tape to create a barcode paint effect.

Also consider temporary facelifts such as a Perspex or glass tabletop, under which you can display photographs or prints, or a stick-on vinyl that could be changed at a later date.

skill level
confident

colour palette
monochrome

time taken
1 hour

covering the table

1 These vinyl floor tiles come in many different colours and patterns. Even better is the fact that they are self-adhesive and very easy to cut.

2 Peel off the backing paper and stick down one tile in a corner position. Then measure the others as you go, laying them on the tabletop and marking in pencil where they need to be cut. Make sure that an uncut edge butts up against another uncut edge as often as possible: the cut edges will look fine along the outside of the table, but no matter how well you trim, your cut edges will never be as good as those cut in the factory and flaws will show when placed against the perfect edge of the table.

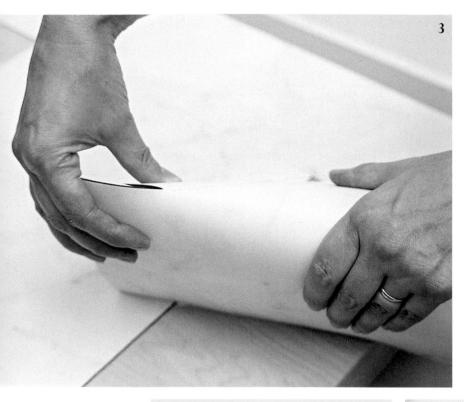

3 Working on the wrong side of the tile, score along your measured line with a craft knife and metal rule – a cutting mat is essential. Bend the tile until the right side splits along the line you have scored.

4 Remove the backing paper and stick the tile in position on the tabletop. Make sure you get it right first time, as the tiles are almost impossible to move once they are stuck down.

quick tip

Using the vinyl tiles is a good budget-conscious option, but you could splash out on a piece of real marble for a sumptuous look. the mirror technique used for the dressing table on page 84 would also look fantastic for this smaller bedside table and would work well in an art-deco inspired bedroom.

beautiful bedrooms gallery

1 Brighten up

Mirror mosaic is a beautiful thing in its own right, but used cleverly it can also be a great decorating tool. Here it's been attached to a doorway, bringing more light into an otherwise dark area.

2 Reflected glory

Vintage mirrors make beautiful and simple display stands for collections of objects, such as the pink-pressed glass seen here.

3 See-through storage

A plain cabinet can be given a simple country-style facelift by painting with a matt cream finish and replacing a door panel with chicken wire. This treatment also works very well for larger items such as wardrobes. If you don't want to see into the cupboard, simply add a lining curtain in a pretty fabric.

4 Embellished headboard

Stapling fabric on top of an existing but uninspiring fabric headboard is an easy task that will give you a whole new look. Try adding embellishments such as buttons and perhaps making up a matching decorative pillow.

5 Fun frosting

A simple pine bedhead has been given a coat of midnight-blue eggshell paint and finished with a layer of glitter glaze – perfect for starry nights!

6 Distressed chest of drawers and mirror

For a gentle look, paint and sand areas of an old chest of drawers to give a distressed effect. This technique is perfect if you want to make a group of mismatched pieces work together.

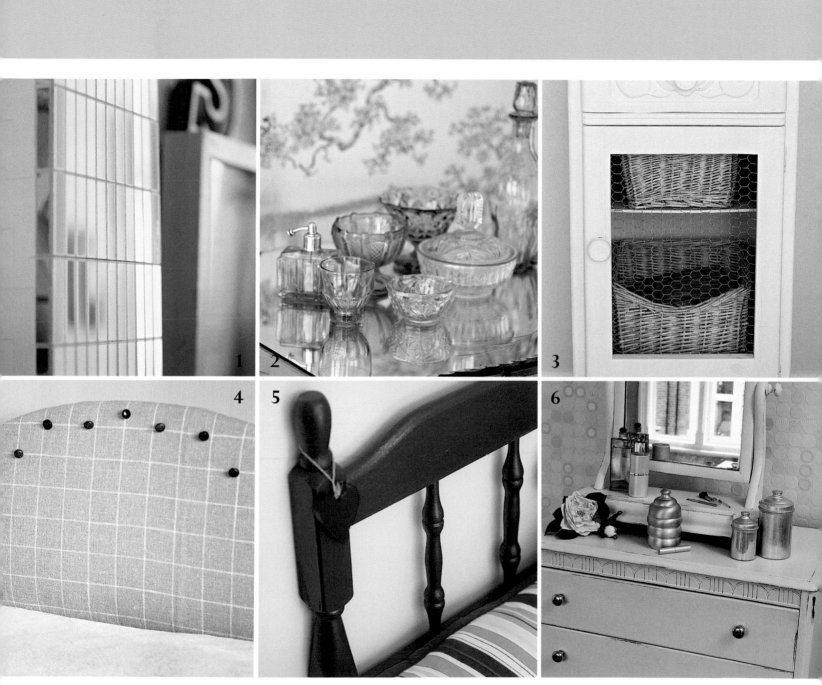

1

2

3

4

5

6

7 Vintage screens

Folding screens are a lovely addition to a bedroom. Cover with a mixture of fabrics in gentle tones and maybe add a hook or two. A decorative hanger will provide a practical finishing touch.

8 Fire screen frame

An old fire screen has been repainted and used to frame a sample length of handpainted wallcovering – great for covering an open fireplace in summer.

9 Wall-mounted bedside lamp

This is the simplest of lights to make, with graph or handmade paper (as seen here) on a basic fitting. It provides a beautiful soft glow. Use low-amp bulbs and don't allow the paper to touch the bulb.

10 Bedside chair

Instead of having a bedside table, why not transform an old chair by painting it red and covering it with tiny white hearts cut out from sticky-backed plastic. A coat of water-based matt varnish will protect your work.

11 Chocolate box chic

Pick up an old art print, cut it to size and then stick it onto a bedside table for a 'shabby chic' look. An old chocolate box lid can be used in the same way. Be sure to finish with a layer or two of varnish to make the surface more hardwearing.

12 Laundry bag and covered hanger

Made from antique embroidered linens and fabric remnants, these bags and hangers also make pretty gifts. Most of us end up with lots of scraps of pretty fabrics and embroidered linens such as hankies, traycloths and table covers that can be used in this way. Buttons can also be recycled into pretty accessories – such as this heart, made by simply threading buttons onto some fine wire.

better bathrooms

No more boring bathrooms! Even the smallest space can benefit from your creative talents: a plainly decorated room, for example, can be livened up by adding a simple little cabinet decorated with naïve handpainted flowers, for a pretty yet subtle effect.

Storage is often the biggest problem in a bathroom – shelves and cabinets positively heave with potions and lotions (for men as well as women!), so think up new ways to store it all.

Useful steals from the kitchen include wine racks and vegetable baskets – even a tea trolley can be called into service as bathroom storage. Space, the ultimate bathroom luxury, might allow you to squeeze in a cuddly armchair covered with fluffy towelling, or to include a toe-comforting rug made from new and vintage terry towelling. If space is at a premium, look for 'multi-tasking' pieces such as sewing stools which double up as storage and a comfy place to sit while painting your toes.

towelling-covered armchair

Q I'm lucky enough to have a large bathroom, but feel it would look cosier with an armchair or some other comfortable seating. Won't upholstery get damp and stain?

A I spotted this on a country house tour and fell in love with the idea of a towelling-covered bathroom chair. Cosy to sit on and hardwearing too, towelling is also a fantastic fabric for the novice upholsterer – it's stretchy, easy to handle, and the pile effectively hides any less-than-perfect beginner's mistakes.

creating bathroom seating

If you love the idea of having bathroom seating but just don't have the space for an armchair, you can still add a touch of comfort by using space-saving ideas. Seats that double up as storage are a perfect example: even a small stool can incorporate a pretty fabric seat. Another option could be to re-sling a folding 'director's chair' with towelling, which could be folded away when not in use.

If you have a family bathroom, removable, washable covers for seating would be a sensible choice. Oilcloth is available in some great colours and patterns, and would be excellent for simply shaped upholstery or cushion pads.

you will need

- Suitable armchair (choose one that is low and simply shaped – old-fashioned nursing chairs are ideal)
- Enough towelling to cover the chair easily – this project used 2.5 m (2¾ yd) of towelling 145 cm (60 in) wide
- Upholstery tacks
- 6 medium-sized buttons (to cover with fabric, or decorative)
- Strong carpet or button thread
- Sewing thread to match towelling

tools

- Fabric scissors
- Staple gun and staples
- Hammer
- Pins
- Medium-gauge needle

skill level
confident

colour palette
blue

time taken
5 hours

covering the armchair

1 When buying a piece of furniture for a facelift, I always give it a detailed check for woodworm, damp or horrible smells indicating rotting upholstery. If I had to re-upholster this chair from scratch it would take a long time, so I gave it a beating with an old-fashioned carpet beater and then cleaned it with upholstery cleaning mousse.

2 Cut a piece of towelling to approximately the same shape as the seat of the chair, adding an extra 8 cm (3 in) of fabric all round for turning in when you attach it to the chair.

3 Lay the fabric onto the seat and, tilting the chair from side to side as you go, fix a few staples through the fabric, attaching it to the underneath of the chair to keep the rest of the fabric in place while you fine tune. Work your way around and around the seat, reducing the gaps between staples with new ones as you go. Run another row around the chair for good measure, ensuring that any excess fabric doesn't flop down and become visible below the seat.

4 Towelling is quite thick, so it is a good idea to make sure that it is held really securely with an upholstery tack every 8 cm (3 in). Hammer in the tacks firmly, but watch out for any woodwork that could be damaged easily while hammering – cover delicate areas with a fabric scrap to protect them. You can now cover other areas of the chair in the same way, leaving the back of the chair as the last area to be covered.

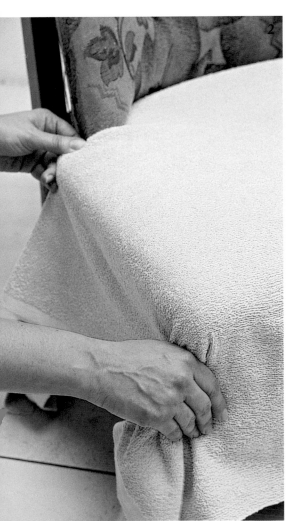

5 A button back adds interest to a chair with a tall back. You could choose to cover the buttons with the same towelling fabric, or use decorative ones such as these mother-of-pearl discs. Decide where to position the buttons and mark with a pin. Using strong button thread, run it through the back of the seat, through the button loop and back again several times, ending with the needle and thread at the back of the chair. Remove the marker pins.

6 Hammer in some tacks around the back of the chair frame, placing them where they won't show through the final fabric covering. Leave the tacks slightly proud of the surface and use them to secure the button threads tightly, pulling them as taut as possible and winding around the tack several times.

7 Finish off everything neatly by stitching down the last piece of fabric, on the back of the chair back, to cover any staples and tacks that have been used to attach the other fabric sections. Because of the pile in the towelling and the loose weave underneath, your stitching does not have to be minute: as long as the thread is exactly the same shade as the towelling, you can use fairly large stitches, secured firmly, and still achieve an excellent finish.

quick tip

If you are a novice upholsterer, towelling is a fantastic fabric and once you are more experienced you can move on to loose-weave linens and cottons. Plains and floral or paisley-style patterns will be fine, but avoid anything with checks or stripes until you are super-confident. It is quite difficult to make these more graphic patterns 'line up' well on a piece or furniture, whereas random patterns tend to be more forgiving.

botanical bathroom cabinet

Q I have a small wooden cabinet that I painstakingly stripped to bare wood a few years ago. However, my tastes have now changed and I would like to paint it. I'm looking for a pretty floral effect, but I can't draw and hate stencils!

A A simple cream background lifted with a dry brush effect in pale blue will make a perfect base for some free-style 'naïve' flowers – anyone can paint these, I promise.

you will need

- Small wooden cabinet
- Several different grades of sandpaper
- Methylated spirits
- 1 litre (2 quarts) multi-purpose primer
- 1 litre (2 quarts) magnolia satin sheen paint
- Sample/tester pot of pale blue satin sheen paint (or other contrast colour of your choice)
- Selection of stencil paints
- Scrap paper
- Small can of water-based matt varnish

tools

- 5 cm (2 in) paintbrush
- Medium-sized artist's brush

using florals

Other ideas for floral motifs could include stamping, découpage (look for flea-market postcards or magazines), gluing on Indian face jewels or tracing copyright-free drawings you like with a soft pencil and transferring them to the painted surface by rubbing from the back. Do re-think stencils as well, as there are some fabulous designs around.

A floral motif could be continued by painting similar flowers onto fabric for window treatments or shower curtains. Country-style floral fabric makes a pretty border for plain white towels, while beautiful hand-stitched flower motifs can be applied to vintage linens or simply framed, to stunning effect.

skill level
easy

colour palette
cream/pastels

time taken
6 hours

painting the cabinet

1 Sand the cabinet with several grades of sandpaper, starting with the coarsest and working through to the finest, to produce the smoothest finish possible. Wipe over with a clean rag dipped in methylated spirits. Apply a coat of primer – don't be tempted to miss out this step, as it's crucial to achieving a good finish.

2 When the primer is completely dry, apply two coats of magnolia satin sheen paint to the cabinet.

3 To give the painted finish more texture, use a 'dry brush' technique. Using pale blue (or other contrast colour) satin sheen paint, barely coat the brush, keeping it very dry. Then just drag the brush gently over the surface of the cabinet, leaving behind a subtle streaked effect.

4 Using stencil paints (I chose beautiful lustre colours) and an artist's brush, practise painting your flower shapes on paper first. Load the brush with paint and gently place the bristles down lengthways on the paper, creating a long oval or petal effect with the paint. Paint three or four of these in a circle to form a flower. Use a different colour to put a small dot in the centre. Try painting several flowers in different sizes. They can – indeed, should – be quite naïve and simple, so don't worry too much.

5 Now try with the real thing. A scattered effect is very pretty. Keep a damp cloth handy to wipe away any errors. When the flowers are dry, finish the whole cabinet with a coat of water-based matt varnish to protect your handiwork.

quick tip

You can recreate this effect on glass with nail varnishes. Use on mirrors, tooth mugs, vases – even a few scattered flowers in the corner of a window will look very sweet.

clothes airer storage

Q I've found a pretty, antique clothes airer that I could use for towels – but to be honest I prefer my towels fresh from a heated rail! Any ideas?

A Bathroom storage is always at a premium, and the addition of some deckchair-striped 'slings' will give this rail a new use as a decorative storage addition to your bathroom.

antique makeovers

This is a lovely antique piece and calls for some restraint. Don't paint an item like this – simply use it for a different purpose until its time comes around again. If you are unsure about whether or not to make over an item, get it valued by an expert. Auction houses and antique shops will be helpful. Wooden pieces such as easy-to-come by pine cupboards and chairs can be painted, stripped and painted again and again over the years, as can be seen in this book. However, a valuable antique will suffer greatly from a mistaken makeover. Make sure you get advice on any item about which you are unsure.

you will need

- Freestanding clothes airer or towel rail
- 2 m (2¼ yd) deckchair fabric
- Tailor's chalk
- 1 m (1¼ yd) leather thonging
- Sewing thread

tools

- Fabric scissors
- Medium-sized sewing needle
- Sewing machine (not essential, but quicker)
- Pins
- Eyelet punch and large eyelets
- Scalpel blade
- Hammer and block of wood

skill level
easy

colour palette
brights

time taken
2 hours

1

making the storage slings

1 Lay the deckchair fabric over the rails of the airer, mark with tailor's chalk and cut to size in two pieces. Leave one top rail free for a towel or clothes. Deckchair fabric is perfect for this, as it is just about the right width for an airer. The seaside theme is also lovely for bathrooms.

2 Hem each end of the long slings by hand or using a sewing machine. Cut out some pockets in which to store items such as face cloths, nail files and sachets – this airer is better suited to smaller items than bulkier objects. Hem all around the pockets, then pin to the slings and stitch into place.

3

quick tip

If space is limited in your bathroom, how about utilizing an old-fashioned ceiling clothes airer? Just like the Victorian originals, they are supplied with pulleys and cord so that, once loaded, they can be pulled up towards the ceiling and out of the way. You could make canvas slings for one of these, but small baskets and bags make a cute eclectic alternative.

3 You will need one eyelet for each corner. Lay the fabric over the airer and mark the positions with tailor's chalk. Packs of large-sized eyelets come with a tool for punching them in. Make a small hole in the fabric with a scalpel blade. Place the eyelet in the hole and rest it on a block of wood. Place the punch on the eyelet and hit with a hammer. Repeat with the rest of the eyelets.

4 Press the slings before hanging in place – be careful if your chosen fabric is new as some versions contain nylon that will shrink if you use too hot an iron.

4

sewing-box storage

Q Help! I'm running out of bathroom storage space and still need to store all my bits and pieces within easy reach. What can I do?

A Old sewing boxes are easy to find and make fabulous storage for all kinds of clutter. Covered with a pretty silk scarf, a stool like this makes the perfect perch for a pedicure.

bathroom storage solutions

Storage is a real issue in a bathroom, and you will see some nifty solutions in the gallery on page 140. Look around your home for other storage ideas that may work in the bathroom. A collection of holiday-style straw baskets hanging from hooks can be as pretty as they are useful, while large preserving jars make great containers for soaps.

skill level
easy

colour palette
lime/lilac

time taken
3 hours

you will need

- Medium-grade sandpaper
- 1 litre (2 quarts) multi-purpose primer
- 1 litre (2 quarts) pearlescent paint
- 0.5 m (¾ yd) calico, wide enough to cover the seat
- Piece of 5 cm (2 in) foam, large enough to pad the seat (if required)
- Silk scarf or fabric, approximately 0.5 m (¾ yd) long and wide enough to cover the seat
- 1.5 m (2 yd) braid
- Other trimmings as required – flowers, ribbon, charms
- Self-cover button
- Sewing thread to match your chosen fabric
- Small button (for fixing)

tools

- 5 cm (2 in) paintbrush
- Craft knife
- Fabric scissors
- Staple gun and staples
- Pins
- Glue gun
- Medium-gauge sewing needle

covering the storage box

1 First remove the legs and sand with medium-grade sandpaper. To paint them, I find it easier to turn the stool upside down and screw in the legs to halfway. Prime first with all-purpose primer, then paint the legs with pearlescent paint for an ultra-feminine flavour. It can take up to four coats to achieve a perfect finish.

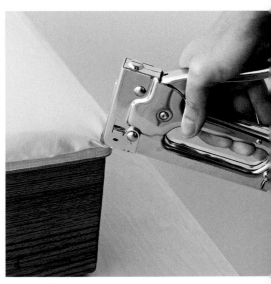

2 If the seat fabric is in good condition and won't show through your new fabric choice, you could leave it in place. Otherwise, remove it using a craft knife. I wanted to preserve the original red lining of this workbox, even though it was slightly damaged, so I left it in place.

3 If the original foam seat is in good condition, simply cover it with plain calico, laid on top of the seat and folded under the seat pad. This will provide a good base for the flimsier fabric of the silk scarf. If necessary, replace the foam seat with a pad of new foam cut to size.

4 Fix one staple at each of the four corners, attaching the pad to the wooden top of the box. This will prevent the pad from slipping.

quick tip

If your bathroom is a splash-happy family space, this silk scarf treatment may not be practical. Keep it in the bedroom, or use a more hardwearing fabric – glazed cottons or chintzes will work, as will bright coloured PVC or oilcloth. If you can find a piece of vintage 1950s towelling, that would make a wonderful fabric seat.

5 Position the silk scarf or fabric on the seat and pin it to the edge of the foam pad. This is to ensure that it doesn't slip while you are stapling it.

6 Open the lid and staple the fabric firmly onto the underside. Don't trim the fabric to size beforehand, as it is much easier to do it after stapling – any untidy edges will be covered with decorative braid later. Make everything as neat as you can: aim to get the staples in a straight line. As you work, keep checking that the fabric is still sitting correctly on top of the lid.

7 Neaten off the inside by gluing braid along the line of staples using a glue gun.

8 If there are any torn or worn areas in the lining, glue on some motifs and ribbon trim to disguise them.

9 Cover a button with your chosen fabric, then thread and secure it through the existing hole (see step 7 on page 97 for precise instructions). If there is no hole for the button, simply staple the centre of the fabric down onto the seat and hand stitch the button on top to hide the staple.

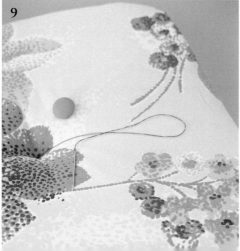

frosted glass window

Q I have made a bathroom in a room that used to be a bedroom, so although I love the windows the glass in them is clear. How can I make them opaque but still pretty and interesting?

A Spray frosting is ideal for this, and even more so if you use a stencil. This not only looks great but is more forgiving: it can be difficult to get a smooth effect with the spray. Stencils are available in many designs, but why not try using objects such as leaves?

you will need

- Scrap wallpaper or newspaper
- Masking tape
- Selection of fern leaves
- Old teatowels
- 1 can of spray-mount adhesive
- 2 cans of frosting spray
- Cotton buds
- Methylated spirits

tools

- Craft knife

frosting alternatives

There are other ways to make a window opaque. Frosted-effect film is very good and you can cut a design into it to add interest – small spots or squares work well. This can also be done in reverse by cutting large circles or squares from frosted self-adhesive vinyl and sticking them onto the window glass.

Another lovely idea is to make a simple wooden frame to fit the window. Stretch fine butter muslin over this frame and then fix it into the window frame with sticky foam pads, to produce a contemporary effect that gives a soft glow to the window.

skill level
confident

colour palette
white

time taken
2 hours

frosting the window

1 It is very important to mask off the area around the window to be treated. The spray will get everywhere and you could end up spending more time clearing up than on the project itself. Wallpaper offcuts are ideal for this – I always keep a box of these handy as a useful 'dust sheet' for all sorts of projects. Newspaper will also do the job. Fix the paper in position with masking tape.

2 Press the fern leaves between old teatowels with an iron set at medium temperature. Iron flat, then coat one side of the leaves with spray-mount adhesive (wallpaper makes a useful dust sheet here, too). Press firmly onto the window pane.

3 It's a good idea to practise using frosting spray on an old bottle or two first. Before you begin, make sure you shake the can really hard for at least one minute. A good tip is to begin and end each spray on the masking paper, not on the glass – this will prevent any thicker areas of spray from accumulating. When you are happy with the technique, progress to the window.

4 When the frosting spray is dry, gently peel away the leaves from the window. A craft knife will help with fiddly bits, and any residue from the spray-mount adhesive can be removed gently with a cotton bud dipped in methylated spirits.

quick tip

I've used a white frosting spray here, but glass frosting sprays are also available in bright jewel colours. Used in small doses, these are ideal if you live in a period property as they can recreate or suggest the appearance of stained glass. If you have a window made up of several small panes, the effect will be very lovely.

paint mosaic mirror

Q I'd love a mosaic mirror, but don't have time to learn the art of mosaic. Is there any way to achieve the same effect more simply?

A This paint-effect technique is the cheat's way to produce a mosaic effect without a tile cutter in sight!

you will need

- Mirror with frame at least 5 cm (2 in) wide
- Masking tape
- Medium-grade sandpaper
- Methylated spirits
- Selection of paints: satin sheen, emulsion, metallic, pearlescent (sample/tester pots are ideal)
- Small can of water-based matt varnish (optional)

tools

- 5 cm (2 in) paintbrush
- Household sponge
- Scissors
- Small plate

styling a mirror

The bathroom is the one room where you can go to town on a mirror and nobody can accuse you of misplaced vanity! This simple wooden-framed mirror could be given any number of different treatments to sit well with your chosen scheme. Use real mirror mosaic pieces for some Hollywood glamour, or bind with rough string for a natural, seaside feel. Trim down an old bamboo blind and attach it to the frame in sections using a glue gun – ideal in an oriental spa-inspired bathroom. For antique appeal, remove the mirror from the frame (for safety's sake) and hammer in some short upholstery tacks randomly around the frame, then distress the wood by simply hitting it with a hammer.

skill level
easy

colour palette
aqua/lilac/gold

time taken
3 hours

2 Apply two coats of your chosen base colour. I used a greeny-blue vinyl silk emulsion. Emulsion paints are fine to use on a project like this, but it is best to seal afterwards with a water-based matt varnish to protect the surface. If you don't want to bother with a varnish top coat, choose water-based satin or eggshell paints.

3 Using scissors, cut a regular household sponge into appropriate-sized stamp pieces with which you will create the mosaic effect. Don't worry too much about making them regular – in fact, the pattern will look best if they are completely random shapes and sizes. You will need one piece of sponge for each different colour.

painting the mirror

1 Mask off the mirror itself with masking tape and sand the frame gently. Clean with a soft cloth dipped in methylated spirits to ensure a smooth and pristine surface.

4 Pour some of your chosen paint onto a small plate. I used a pearlescent paint, as I like the different reflections and texture that it produces. Dip one of the sponge pieces gently into the paint and then press down firmly (but not too hard) onto the frame, to create one mosaic piece. Continue to build up the pattern in this way – again, random is best.

quick tip

Making your own stamps can be very effective and great fun. Good old-fashioned potato printing is definitely worth revisiting and looks great with bright colours. A swirl of string glued onto a block of wood or even a piece of scrunched-up newspaper can also create wonderful effects.

5 A gold metallic paint adds another dimension to this project with its light-reflective qualities. Follow the same procedure as in step 4, leaving some areas as the base colour.

6 If necessary (see step 2), apply a final coat of water-based matt varnish to protect the surface.

better bathrooms gallery

1 Wine rack for bottles

A wine rack painted with a pale woodwash is a good storage solution for all those bottles of (bath) bubbly.

2 Wire vegetable baskets

Another effective storage idea is to recycle hanging vegetable baskets into hanging toiletries baskets instead.

3 Roller towel rails

A great idea for children is these roller towels, made using kitchen roll dispensers and hand towels cut to size and sewn into a loop.

4 Fabric shower curtain

Almost any fabric you choose can be lined with cheap plastic and transformed into a shower curtain to match the scheme in your bathroom.

5 Wheelie trolley

An old tea trolley is transformed into stylish storage with the addition of a subtle gold paint effect applied to the trays of the trolley.

6 Towelling rug

This patchwork towelling bath mat is both practical and fun. You can use bath towels, vintage fabric and fabric from the roll to make it. If you have a slippery bathroom floor, attach non-slip rubber pads to the back.

index

acknowledgements

Executive Editors Sarah Tomley and Katy Denny
Project Editor Kate Tuckett
Executive Art Editor Joanna MacGregor
Designer Beverly Price, one2six creative
Photographer Frazer Cunningham
Senior Production Controller Martin Croshaw